THE MOST BEAUTIFUL CHINESE MINDS SERIES

“最美中国人”丛书

ORDINARY PEOPLE: LIVING A VIBRANT LIFE

平凡老百姓：把日子过出精气神儿

“最美中国人”丛书编委会 编著

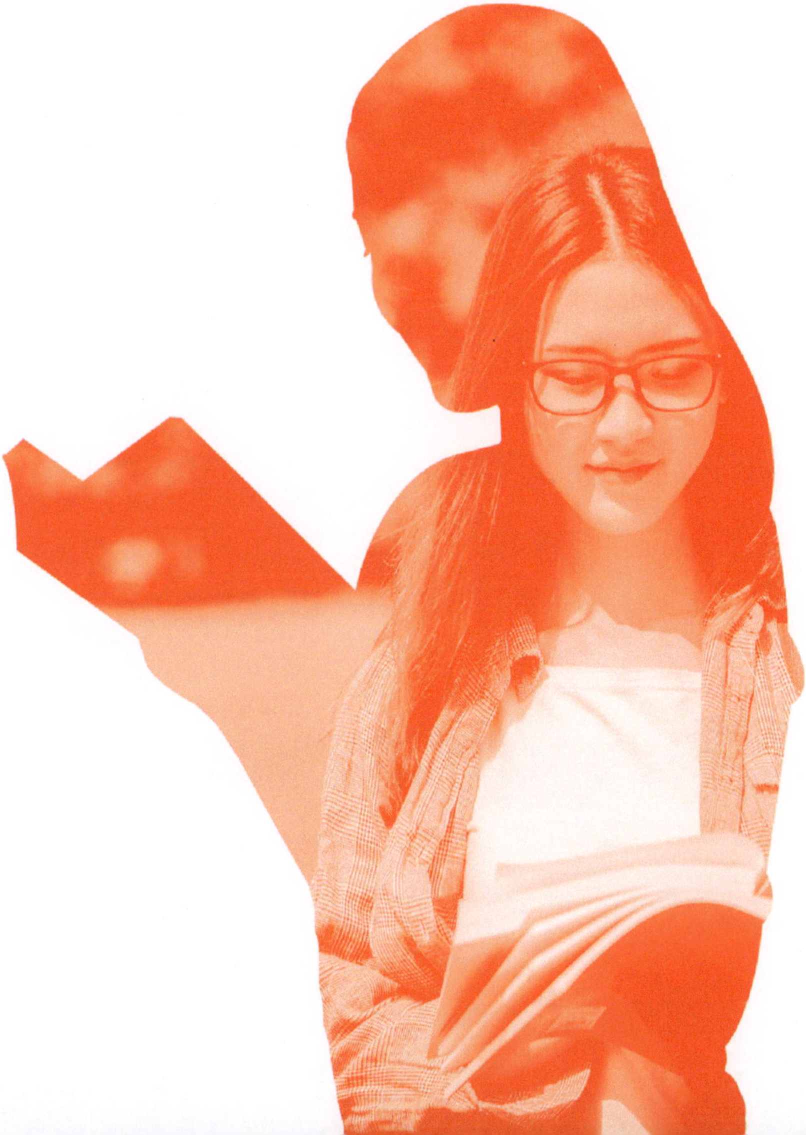

SinolinguA
华语教学出版社

First Edition 2022
Second Printing 2022

ISBN 978-7-5138-2193-3
Copyright 2022 by Sinolingua Co., Ltd
Published by Sinolingua Co., Ltd
24 Baiwanzhuang Street, Beijing 100037, China
Tel: (86)10-68320585, 68997826
Fax: (86)10-68997826, 68326333
http://www.sinolingua.com.cn
E-mail: hyjx@sinolingua.com.cn
Facebook: www.facebook.com/sinolingua
Printed by Beijing Hucais Culture Communication Co., Ltd.

Printed in the People's Republic of China

"最美中国人"丛书编委会

主 编

王君校　韩　晖

张　坤　毛　浩　董　时

编 委

韩　颖　付　眉　刘小琳　张　超

黄　勇　许　革　吴晓东　付豪杰　王荣华

编 务

马博韬

Editorial Board

Chief Editors
Wang Junxiao Han Hui
Zhang Kun Mao Hao Dong Shi

Editors
Han Ying Fu Mei Liu Xiaolin Zhang Chao
Huang Yong Xu Ge Wu Xiaodong Fu Haojie Wang Ronghua

Assistant Editor
Ma Botao

前言

"最美中国人"丛书以中英对照的形式向外国读者讲述新时代中国人民的奋斗故事。本丛书用细致生动的笔触介绍了志愿者、创业者、90后、普通百姓和老年人这几个不同人群中的典型故事,反映出中国人民在中国共产党的领导下实现全面小康的逐梦历程。丛书一共五册,分别是《志愿者:让爱传递到每个角落》《创业者:幸福是奋斗出来的》《出彩90后:我的青春不后悔》《平凡老百姓:把日子过出精气神儿》《中国"传家宝":那些可爱的老人们》,每册包含八到十个真实故事。为了让外国读者更加直观地了解中国社会的发展和人民生活的巨大变迁,丛书除了文字故事之外,部分故事还配有视频二维码,读者扫描二维码即可观看与文章配套的人物故事视频。

FOREWORD

"The Most Beautiful Chinese Minds" is a book series for international readers featuring stories of Chinese people from all walks of life in today's China. Presented in both Chinese and English, the series reveals the vivid and personal stories of the everyday lives of volunteers, entrepreneurs, post-90s youth, ordinary people and senior citizens as they strive to realize their own dreams and the national dream of building a moderately prosperous society in all aspects under the leadership of the Chinese Communist Party. The series includes five volumes: *Volunteers: Making the World a Better Place*, *Entrepreneurs: Striving for Happiness*, *Born in the 90s: Never Regretting Our Youth*, *Ordinary People: Living a Vibrant Life*, and *Charming Seniors: Keeping Up with the Times*. Each volume consists of eight to ten true stories about real people. It is a must-read for those wishing to better understand the true experiences of everyday Chinese people in today's China and the remarkable changes taking place in their lives. We have also provided QR codes for some stories which can link to online videos about the people from the passages.

目录 | CONTENTS

点燃苗寨的火塘 ······2
Lighting the Miao Fire Pit ······9

丁丁和母亲一起奔跑的人生 ······17
The Life Marathon of a Mother and Her Son ······28

宿管员霞姐的 N 个角色 ······39
The Multiple Roles of a Dormitory Supervisor ······48

从震墟中起身，微笑向前 ······58
Rising from the Earthquake Ruins ······70

满地六便士，他抬头看见月亮 ······82
Sixpence Is Everywhere, But He Looks Up and Sees the Moon ······92

北漂国学老师之"道" ······104
A Teacher of Traditional Chinese Culture in Beijing ······112

小保安闯出大名堂 ······120
An Ambitious Security Guard ······127

火雷兄弟，江湖再见 ······136
See You Again, Fire and Thunder Brothers ······146

点燃苗寨的火塘

Lighting the Miao Fire Pit

作者：李玥
翻译：张乐

点燃苗寨的火塘

2015年年末,在贵州省黄平县的文化中心,龙阿朵当着县文化中心负责人杨德的面给自己"挖了一个坑":用半年的时间把苗寨的火塘搬上北京的舞台。通常,这样一台演出可能要花费六七百万元,但龙阿朵只有一百万的经费。即便参与过北京奥运会开幕式导演、曾与张艺谋合作过"印象"系列演出,龙阿朵还是有点儿"忐忑"。

2016年,龙阿朵花了5个月时间创作和执导的苗族舞蹈诗《巫卡调恰》(苗语,意为外婆的歌谣)在北京连演三场,每场都座无虚席,专程从陕西、海南等地赶来的观众涌向舞台与演员拥抱。有人评价,剧中的火塘"点燃"了苗人的乡愁,"烧热"了对故乡苗寨的记忆。

火塘是苗族人生活的中心,吃饭、取暖、议事大都围绕火塘进行。苗族人家家户户都有火塘,生生不息,是一个民族温暖的磁场。

Lighting the Miao Fire Pit
点燃苗寨的火塘

龙阿朵左手的银镯子是现在她身上唯一的苗族符号。这是外婆留给她的，她时不时转动手腕上的银镯，仿佛正在跟外婆进行灵魂的对话。小时候，龙阿朵挨着做刺绣的外婆靠在火塘边，听她唱古歌，苗族的历史和家风在古歌中传承。

舞蹈诗《巫卡调恰》时长70分钟，所有故事都围绕火塘展开：火塘上方祭放着谷种，外婆坐在火塘边为孙女穿上苗族盛装——百褶裙、围腰、凤冠，哼唱古歌讲述苗族的传说。

2014年冬天，龙阿朵受邀回到家乡。当她裹着棉大衣无意中走进镇里的小学时，发现学生只穿着几件单衣御寒。宿舍里，学生用破棉絮代替被褥，有些床铺干脆垫着稻草。她边抹泪边在朋友圈求助。看着棉衣棉鞋从全国各地涌来，这位导演仅仅开心了5分钟便开始琢磨作为艺术家去扶贫究竟能做什么。

"虽然文化丰富，但我们缺人才，没有走得出去的好作品。"一直渴望外援的县文化中心负责人杨德与龙阿朵一拍即合。他给这位文艺志愿者提了个要求，演员要从当地找，避免外来演员一走节目就死的窘境。"如果需要，我愿意扎在这里搞创作。"龙阿朵立下军令状。

十天后，龙阿朵组织了一支文艺扶贫队伍再次回到黄平。一开始就碰到了难题。龙阿朵以为找演员不难，她记忆里的黄平人"会说话就会唱歌，能走路就能跳舞"，每个寨子的马郎坡是青年男女对歌谈情的地方，家家户户的火塘旁男女老少和着芦笙起舞，通宵达旦。然而，现实和这些离开苗寨30多年的记忆完全对不上号。苗寨的火塘渐渐熄灭了，马郎坡不再有歌声。

寨子里的老人摇摇头，"现在的人谈恋爱不唱歌，看看电影吃吃饭就结婚了。"保留在农耕文化里的火塘渐渐退出楼房里的城市生活，饭店里的聚会难见欢歌起舞。外出打工的年轻人能多学几首苗族大歌再走成为一位年近八旬的古歌传承人最大的心愿。

为了选演员，她满大街游荡，见到长得顺眼的姑娘小伙儿就立刻冲上去询问会不会跳舞。最终入选的20位演员分别是县城服装店售货员、餐饮店服务员、外出打工者以及7岁男孩的妈妈。这位准备就地开展文艺培训的导演向演员竖起一根手指，"只要有'真'，我就能点燃你们。"

未受过专业辅导的演员就在没有把杆、镜子，临时用木板搭起的舞台上排练，每天训练9小时。1小时的训练强度等同于做15分钟平板支撑，而普通人坚持两分钟都很难。5个月里，每位演员都踢坏了好几双舞蹈鞋。

王小英因为训练瘦了20斤，"我第一次知道我也能跳舞，我的身份可以不只是谁的妈妈、谁的老婆，而是把苗族宣传出去的人"。

"我就是迁徙的人，演得出剧里留恋故乡的眼神"。演员袁金培高中毕业后随县里的务工潮去广东一家服装厂打工。为了赶工，他曾三天没合眼。

"你们每一个人都是主演。"龙阿朵告诉演员，"把火塘当成民族的生命之源，去呵护、去爱。"

她做了个道具火塘给演员示范，身体前倾，对着柴火轻轻吹气，注视火苗起伏，像感受心脏的跳动。她跪在火塘边说："这是用身体语言来表达火塘文化。"

这是一部关于苗族历史的舞蹈诗。涿鹿大战失败后，蚩尤率领苗族先民从黄河中下游地区向西、向南迁徙。《巫卡调恰》就是通过坐在火塘边的外婆吟唱古歌来呈现这一段历史。扮演灵魂的演员踩着象征黄河的黄绸倒退行走，面朝灯光走向黑暗，眼睛始终望着故乡。

在山里，龙阿朵把每天的黄昏时间留给自己思考。她看到一朵云的形状像极了苗族祖先蚩尤，蓄长须，一头乱发。她还发现一只苗族人奉为图腾的蝴蝶一直跟了她两个小时。这位导演逢人便讲这些经历，期待对方回一句"你注定要做这件事"。

生活在仅有一家电影院的黄平，原本能歌善舞的苗族人平日里接触最多的"表演"只剩下广场舞。看完《巫卡调恰》的排练，有观众很疑惑："这哪是戏，这和以前坐在火塘边听老人讲故事一个样。"一位认为跳舞是不务正业的父亲看到女儿"一板一眼把苗族演活了"，寡言的汉子也学着城里人的样子买了花给女儿捧场。有一次在饭店,坐在龙阿朵对面的妇女认出了她,掏出钱就要帮她付账,"我看过你的剧,给我们苗族立功了!"

苗族老乡都说好,但能否得到业界的认可,龙阿朵心里有个问号。5个月封闭训练结束后,龙阿朵邀请母校北京舞蹈学院副院长赵铁春观摩。在群山环抱的简陋场地看完演出,她曾经的老师评价这部"简朴的"舞蹈诗"找到了传统和现代、民族和时尚的结合点",并当场决定邀请《巫卡调恰》团队去北京舞蹈学院演出。

苗寨的火塘在北京点燃。当灯光亮起,演员抄起板凳,围着火塘和着古歌起舞。

"你们太了不起了,竟然把苗族的火塘点起来了。"一谢幕,有观众哭着拥抱演员。杨德冲上舞台,隔着人群高高竖起大拇指,向总导演龙阿朵喊道:"这一生做成这么一件事,真的值了!"

龙阿朵没想到,北京演出结束后,在她的家乡,火塘越烧越旺。

从不过苗族节日的一位女演员向母亲提

出同去参加今年的芦笙节，还特意把她曾经认为"很土"的盛装翻出来穿上。"是苗族让我特别骄傲。"她说。还有一位女演员每天念叨最多的就是排练的场景。家人一度认为她"丢了魂"，还请苗族巫师为她做法事。原本打算演完《巫卡调恰》就继续去广东打工的男演员决定不走了，因为"县里的文化值得挖掘，值得留下"。听到这个消息，全舞团的人都眉开眼笑。

2017年，《巫卡调恰》作为贵州省推荐的两个节目之一参加了9月在北京举办的全国少数民族文艺会演。龙阿朵还把这部剧留在了黄平，每周驻场演出，真正变成了宣传苗族文化的一个窗口，实现了中国文联"文艺扶贫奔小康"的目标。

北京演出谢幕时有观众问她，你花了不到半年时间带着业余演员从零开始原创作品，做这个决定时你没觉得给自己挖了一个坑吗？这位导演转了转戴在左手的苗族银手镯，"人生难得有给自己挖坑的冲动。"

Lighting the Miao Fire Pit

It was the end of 2015. Director Long Aduo was standing in the culture center of Huangping County, Guizhou Province with Yang De, director of the culture center. She had dug herself into a hole. She had agreed to choreograph a show to be performed in Beijing in half a year's time. Normally, to prepare for such a performance would cost six or seven million yuan. But she only had a budget of one million yuan. Even for a director who had been part of the directing team of the 2008 Beijing Olympic opening ceremony and had worked with Zhang Yimou on his "Impression" shows, she was quite uneasy about this seemingly impossible challenge.

For the next five months, Long Aduo created and rehearsed the show, a Miao epic dance show called *Ballads from Grandma*. The show featured stories and legends about Miao culture which were usually told around the fire pit, the centerpiece of Miao social gatherings. In May 2016, the show debuted in Beijing to a packed house for the three performances. People came from Shaanxi, Hainan and other provinces and regions to see it. Afterwards, some audience members even went on stage to hug the dancers. As someone commented, the fire pits in the show had "kindled" Miao people's longing for home, and "warmed up" the memories of their hometowns.

The *huotang* — or fire pit is the centerpiece of Miao social life.

They arrange their daily activities around it, such as dining, keeping warm, and discussing important family matters. The fire pit in every household is like a cultural magnet for the Miao people, a heritage that has been passed down from generation to generation.

The silver bracelet Long Aduo wore around her left wrist is a typical Miao design. Her grandmother left it to her. Every now and then she touches and turns the bracelet, which she said reminded her of her grandmother, and also of the time when she would sit next to her and listen to her sing ancient songs while doing embroidery. Through these songs, Miao heritage and traditions get passed down through generations.

Ballads from Grandma is a reflection of these memories. The 70-minute performance features a grandmother sitting next to a fire pit humming ancient songs to her granddaughter sitting beside her. Sacrificial millet seeds are placed over the fire pit as the grandmother dresses her granddaughter in beautiful Miao clothing including a pleated skirt, an embroidered apron, and a phoenix headdress.

In the winter of 2014, Long Aduo went back to her hometown of Huangping Village. One day, she accidentally wandered into a primary school. She noticed that the students there had no warm clothing during the winter, while she was wearing a thick coat. In their dorm, some students used worn cotton wadding as blankets, and some even used straw as a mattress. In tears, she posted a message online to ask for help. She was happy to soon see thick clothing and warm shoes mailed in from all across China. However, she knew that as a director and an artist, she needed to do more to try to help lift people here out of poverty.

"Although our culture is rich, we lack the talents who have the know-how to produce works that can appeal to a larger audience." Yang De, director of the county culture center, was looking for someone with this kind of expertise. He and Long Aduo shared similar views, and decided to work together. He suggested that the performers should be local people, as the show would be jeopardized if performers left. "If needed, I'd like to stay here to produce the show," Long Aduo promised.

Ten days later, Long Aduo led a team to Huangping Village to begin searching for performers, but she quickly ran into a problem. In her childhood memories, people in Huangping "could sing when they learned to speak, and could dance as soon as they could walk." In her memories, it was common for young lovers to sing to each other. In each household, all the family members, young or old, would dance around the fire pit in the evening to the sounds of reed-pipe wind instruments, even all through the night. But thirty years later, things had changed. The fire pits were not lit. No love songs were heard.

When asked, the elderly in the village shook their heads and told her, "Nowadays, people no longer sing to each other on dates. They go get dinner and a movie. Then they tie the knot." The fire pit that had once been the center of Miao agrarian culture was slowly disappearing as apartment buildings rose up in growing cities. People seldom sang or danced during get-togethers held in restaurants. For a local nearly eighty-year-old singer, his greatest wish was that young Miao people could learn a few more Miao traditional songs before they left their hometowns to work in the cities.

Long Aduo scoured the streets to find dancers. She would approach every good-looking young person and ask if they could dance. The final twenty people selected were from many backgrounds: salespeople at clothing shops, waiters and waitresses, migrant workers, and the mother of a seven-year-old boy. Upon gathering them, Director Long Aduo raised her index finger and said to them, "As long as there is truth in you, I can ignite you."

On a temporary stage made of wood planks, the untrained dancers started rehearsing without poles or mirrors. They trained nine hours a day. The training was very intense, with one hour's training as demanding as doing 15 minutes of the "plank pose" exercise, where a normal person could barely undergo two minutes. During the five months of rehearsals, every dancer wore out several pairs of shoes.

Dancer Wang Xiaoying lost 20 kilograms during rehearsals. "For the first time in my life, I realized that I could dance, and my identity was not just tied to being a mom or a wife, but also someone who can show the Miao culture to many people."

"I work far away from home, so I know how such a person's eyes can reveal their homesickness," said performer Yuan Jinpei. He went to work in a garment factory in Guangzhou after graduating from high school. On one occasion, he worked three days and three nights straight to meet a factory deadline.

"Each of you is a lead actor," Long Aduo told the actors. "Treat the fire pit as the source of life of our people; protect it and love it."

She demonstrated in front a prop representing the fire pit. She leaned forward and blew gently into the firewood and watched the flames dance upward like the beating of a heart. She knelt down next to it and said, "Use the body this way to express the culture of the Miao fire pit."

The show was an epic dance celebrating the history of the Miao people. After a major defeat around 4,600 BCE, legendary Miao leader Chiyou led the ancestors of the Miao people to relocate westward and southward from the middle and lower reaches of the Yellow River. *Ballads from Grandma* recreates this history. As the grandmother sings the ancient songs beside the fire pit, dancers appear, representing the souls from the past, walking backwards on yellow silk which symbolizes the Yellow River. They face the light and the direction of their hometown, and fade into darkness.

At dusk, Long Aduo would spend time alone thinking in the mountains every day. She once saw clouds resembling their ancestor Chiyou with a long beard and bushy hair. She also once noticed a butterfly — the symbol of Miao culture — following her for two hours. She would share these moments with many people, in the hope that they would say something encouraging like "You're destined to do this."

Huangping only had one cinema. So, for the musical Miao people, the most popular entertainment was probably the group dances in the public squares. After seeing a rehearsal of *Ballads from Grandma*, some viewers were doubtful. For them, it seemed too common. "How can you call this a show?" they'd comment. "It's just like the old days when you sat beside the fire pit and listened to a story." But there were more encouraging voices. A father who assumed that dancing was not a proper career saw his daughter "acting out the essence of the Miao people." The reserved man brought flowers to his daughter at the show. One time in a restaurant, Long Aduo was recognized, and the person offered to pay for her meal. "I've seen your show," the person said. "It's the pride of our Miao people!"

Even though she seemed to have the support of her fellow Miao people, Long Aduo was not sure how the art community would react. After five months of intensive training, she invited Zhao Tiechun, her teacher and vice president of the Beijing Dance Academy, to watch their performance. On a simple stage surrounded by mountains, Mr. Zhao watched their performance and commented that the epic dance was "straightforward" and "a recipe to integrate the traditional, the modern, the ethnic, and the fashionable." He decided on the spot to invite the troupe to perform at the Beijing Dance Academy.

The Miao fire pit was lit in Beijing. When the lights came on, the dancers picked up their stools and danced around the fire pit to the ancient songs.

"You're amazing. You've re-lit the fire pit of the Miao ethnic group," people said. After the curtain call, some audience members came up to embrace the actors in tears. Yang De also ran to the stage and gave a thumbs-up to Director Long Aduo, shouting to her over a crowd, "To accomplish such a thing in one's life — it was completely worth it!"

To Long Aduo's surprise, after their performance in Beijing, the show moved south to her home province, where the fire pit began burning even more vigorously.

One of the dancers used to be indifferent when it came to Miao festivals, but now she wanted to go to the Lusheng (reed pipe) Festival with her mother. She even put on her ethnic costume for the occasion. "I'm proud to be a member of Miao," she said. Another dancer couldn't stop talking about the scenes from their rehearsal. Her family thought she had been "possessed" and asked a Miao shaman for help. Another actor who had worked in Guangdong decided to stay, as he believed it was a worthy cause for him to stay to explore and celebrate the culture. The entire troupe was overjoyed upon hearing the news.

Ballads from Grandma was one of the two programs recommended by Guizhou Province to be performed at the China Ethnic Minorities Art Festival in September 2017. In addition, the show went on to be staged in Huangping every week, which became a window into Miao culture and part of the efforts to help local people seek a better life through art.

During the curtain call in Beijing, an audience member asked Long Aduo if she felt she had dug herself into a hole when she had decided to create a new show with amateur actors in less than half a year's time. She touched her silver Miao bracelet and said, "It's a rare thing in life to do something like this that you truly believe in."

Ordinary People: Living a Vibrant Life
平凡老百姓：把日子过出精气神儿

Scan for a Video

丁丁和母亲一起奔跑的人生

The Life Marathon of a Mother and Her Son

作者：朱娟娟
翻译：薛彧威

丁丁和母亲一起奔跑的人生

2017年5月，美国波士顿，中国留学生丁丁刚从哈佛大学法学院毕业，转身又投入到美国司法考试的复习准备中。29年前，因宫内缺氧面临窒息，丁丁一出生被诊断为重度脑瘫。在五份病危通知书以及"将来非瘫即傻"的预言面前，妈妈邹翃燕选择将他留下。2007年，丁丁以660分的成绩考入北京大学环境科学与工程学院；2015年，丁丁考入哈佛。丁丁说，能做妈妈的儿子"很幸运"。

邹翃燕是一名单亲妈妈，对她来说，这29年，是一场与儿子一起奔跑的"人生马拉松"。

1988年7月18日的凌晨，"发令枪"响了。

孩子生下来的揪心一幕刻在邹燕的记忆中：孩子全身发紫，不哭也不闹，双眼紧闭；转院抢救，孩子小小的鼻孔一个插着输氧管，一个插着鼻饲管；护士来打针，扎不进，汗珠一滴滴落在孩子皱巴巴的脸上，孩子还是没丝毫反应，眉头都不皱一下。

"重度脑瘫，没抢救价值了，救下来也非瘫即傻。"医生隔会儿再来说一遍，"为了孩子和你自己的未来，仔细想想，下决心吧。"

那晚，邹翃燕把儿子搂在怀里，一夜无眠。江汉平原夏夜的燥热，似乎与她无关。她全部的注意力覆盖在儿子耷拉的眼皮上，"我是妈妈，你看看我呀""这世界挺美的，你好不容易走一遭，睁开眼看看"……

凌晨5点，孩子终于有了反应——哼唧了一下，像小猫一样，随后终于哭了。医生说，能哭出来，命就保住了，但今后的路必将"痛苦艰辛又漫长"。

她给孩子起名丁丁（第二个字念"zhēng"），即是因为她想起《诗经》里"伐木丁丁，鸟鸣嘤嘤"的诗句，大树砍伐都有响动，她希望他至少能在这世界留一点声响。

让丁丁活下来，是第一个层次。怎样让

他活好一点？这个"好"，照邹翃燕的理解：肢体各项功能最好逐渐接近正常人，要有一技之长，要有阳光的心态，能在有所作为中体味活着的趣味与价值。

丁丁1岁前检测，智力没问题，但轻偏瘫，左脚活动不灵，有运动障碍。他总是流口水，双手没力气握不住东西，两岁半才勉强学走路。

邹翃燕带着丁丁四处求医。湖北中医学院疑难杂症科医生告诉她，脑瘫按摩治疗，3～6岁是黄金时期，但需持之以恒，科学训练。

每周按摩3次，邹翃燕下了班，骑自行车带丁丁去。路并不好走。一次下大雪，自行车倒在水坑里，他滚到了地上。妈妈把他扶起来，车倒了；车扶起来，他又倒了……他哭了，妈妈也哭了。

娘儿俩泥猴儿似地到了医院。医生感叹，"这天气，以为你俩不会来了。""就是下刀子，也要来。"妈妈斩钉截铁。

每次按摩一个小时，背部的皮被捏起来一点点捻过，3岁的丁丁疼得哇哇直哭、咬牙切齿，他求妈妈"能不能不去"。

邹翃燕很清楚，有了一次，就有第二次，"如果有很多理由，我就会不断原谅自己"，那就没法坚持了。她必须保持理性——尽最大努力，为丁丁的命运再多争取一点点逆转。

伴随一路艰辛，希望就像是清晨的阳光挣脱云翳，最初是一丝一丝，后来是一缕一缕。

5岁多，丁丁终于可以双脚同时离地跳一下了。那天，丁丁在院子里逮着人就大喊，"你看我会跳、我会跳！我跳给你看！"那天丁丁兴奋的样子，似乎仍在邹翃燕眼前。

丁丁小时候学握笔、用筷子都是艰巨工程，光这两样，他就学了一年。长大后，他感谢有这样明智的妈妈，一桌人吃饭，如果他不用筷子，别人会好奇，还得跟人解释自己脑瘫，麻烦又伤自尊。

丁丁行动不便，但也形成了做事专注的性格特点。

因为手指不够灵活，上小学三年级前，丁丁写字慢。邹翃燕为丁丁申请考试延时，一开始20分钟，后来逐渐缩短到5分钟，四年级后，丁丁写字速度赶上来了，延时停止。

"妈妈从不辅导我作业。"丁丁说，小学开学，妈妈送给自己《新华字典》，有不认识的字，妈妈就一句话"自己查字典去"，无形中，独立学习的能力得以锻炼。

读三年级时，老师要求家长出试卷给孩子做，做完还要检查、打分。邹翃燕从来不出，都是鼓励丁丁自己出、自己做。邹翃燕统统不检查就打100分。

一次，丁丁回来闷闷不乐，"妈妈，你今天被我们老师批评了，我做的题明明有两道错的你还打100分，老师说你不负责。"

"我以后还会天天给你打100分。"邹燕很淡定，卷子既然自己出、自己做，还好意思做不对？我们行动比同学慢一点，那更要保证正确率呀。

从此，丁丁养成了做一道题就尽量做仔细做对的习惯，正确率越来越高。邹翃燕后来总结，丁丁能考取北大、哈佛，与小时候养成的这些学习习惯不无关系。

"学霸"丁丁也有迷茫的时候。

初中,丁丁保送进了一所省重点中学。但开学才几天,正在出差的邹翃燕就接到丁丁电话,"哭着说不想上学了,要我回去办退学手续。"

原来,军训练习高抬腿,丁丁站不稳,有同学也做不好,教官只批评别人。同学质疑时,年轻的教官脱口而出"他是脑瘫"。有的孩子便编顺口溜骂丁丁是"茗"(武汉羞辱人方言——记者注),还将他的文具盒传来传去,嘲笑他,捉弄他。

邹翃燕连夜坐了30多个小时火车赶回武汉。课间,邹翃燕走上讲台。她说,同学们,你们都很幸运、很健康,可丁丁身体不好。你们长大后,可以当运动员、当兵、当飞行员、去做任何喜欢的事与工作,丁丁不行,他只有读书一条路。现在,他不想上学了,那他以后该怎么办呢?还会开心吗?大家是不是应该理解他、包容他、帮助他呀?台下,寂静无声。

那学期期末考试,丁丁考了全年级第一,从此再没受过欺负。长大后的丁丁这样形容这段往事："虽然妈妈出面一个顶俩，但一辈子需要妈妈这样操心也不行。"

在丁丁心目中，妈妈对自己总是循循善诱，"教育小孩用的是智慧"。

高二时，他一度成绩十分不理想，他很失落，反问妈妈：为什么一定要考名校？

妈妈带他去东湖边看房子。在一楼，妈妈问，"能看到东湖吗？"

"不能。"

上到六楼，"能看到吗？"

"能。"

"看得清楚吗？形容一下。"

"不是很清楚，就像一个小手绢。"

到了20层，母子俩眼前，东湖水面开阔，尽收眼底。

"这才是东湖真正的样子啊。"妈妈告诉他，东湖的样子是客观存在的，人在不同的平台，视野不同，看到的景象才有所不同，站得高了，才有可能看到你想要看到的。

很快，丁丁找回状态。2007年，他以660分考入北大环境科学与工程学院。

经过多年坚持康复训练，丁丁的身体也越来越接近正常人，总体不影响生活，只有穿针引线、科学实验的精细动作等无法完成。2011年，他放弃喜欢的环科专业，改修国际法，并顺利保送至北大国际法学院读研。

硕士毕业后，丁丁在国内一家知名互联网公司做法务。工作了一年，他感觉还想继续深造。对于哈佛，他原本"不敢想"。

邹翃燕清楚丁丁的情况：曾两次获国家奖学金，被评为北大三好学生、北大优秀毕业生、北京市优秀毕业生，读研期间也成绩优异。她特意咨询了丁丁的导师，鼓励丁丁去试一试。

原本哈佛给丁丁发了拒信，但在看了导师推荐信后，又给他发了录取通知书，而且是免托福成绩。

把脑瘫孩子送进了哈佛，邹翃燕不觉得自己伟大。她更愿意把自己定义为"一个为了孩子不断成长进步的妈妈"，自己绝不只是这场马拉松的陪跑者，她也是运动员。伴随医生当年断言的"痛苦艰辛又漫长"，她也收获了力量与快乐。

培养儿子的同时，邹翃燕从未放松对事业的追求：她是副教授，是武汉市教坛新秀、武汉市青年女教职工标兵、武汉市首届优秀青年教师、武汉市学科带头人，也是湖北省礼仪学会副会长、高级形象管理师。

在邹翃燕家中，一幅画挂了30年：长着翅膀的小天使依偎在妈妈怀里。这幅画是邹翃燕怀孕时买的，后来发现丁丁有缺陷，她也觉得，丁丁跟任何一个孩子一样，是一个家庭的希望，"折翼的天使……还是天使啊！"

对妈妈的一往直前，丁丁用行动表达敬佩：丁丁小时候对穿别人的旧衣服从来没意见；为节约路费，除寒暑假外他都不回家；读研时，他经常顶烈日从北大走到清华，因为清华食堂饭菜更便宜。

邹翃燕感觉，母子俩就像一个大写的"人"字，丁丁是一撇，她是一捺，相互支撑，相伴相生。从死神手里抢回一条命，打破"非傻即瘫"的断言，考进北大与哈佛，这些都只是一路上的站点，"人生的马拉松没有终点"。

丁丁的下一站，是近期备战的美国司法考试。他每天复习8～12个小时。"考试很难。"他也发愁。

邹翃燕的下一站，是希望为更多的脑瘫患儿提供一点儿帮助。

中国现有600万左右脑瘫患者，绝大多数是儿童。在中国，公众对脑瘫的认知停留在较低层次，最常见的就是将之与智力发育不良划上等号，事实上，只有不足40%的脑瘫患者存在智力缺陷。很多人并没有正确认识到脑瘫的普遍性和可治疗性。中国一些脑瘫孩子缺乏有效治疗，甚至很难存活到成年。

丁丁考上北大后，陆续有朋友将邹翃燕介绍给一些脑瘫儿家庭。这对母子决定把他们的故事告诉大家，给同样境遇的孩子和家长一些鼓励，让他们有信心走下去。

邹翃燕建了个微信群，大家可以相互鼓励、交流治疗方法。"多一些坚持，这些孩子或许都能成为可以自立的人。"

The Life Marathon of a Mother and Her Son

In May 2017, Ding Zheng, a new Chinese graduate from Harvard Law School, began his preparation for the Uniform Bar Exam (UBE). Twenty-nine years ago, he suffered suffocation as a baby due to intrauterine hypoxia and was diagnosed with severe brain paralysis upon birth. In the face of her son's five critical condition notices and the prediction that he could become paralyzed or have learning disabilities in the future, Ding Zheng's mother Zou Hongyan made a decision to keep the baby and bring him up. In 2007, he enrolled in the College of Environmental Sciences and Engineering at Peking University with 660 points. Eight years later, Ding Zheng was admitted to Harvard University. He said, "I'm very fortunate to be my mom's son!"

As a single mother, Zou had been running a "life marathon" with her son over the past 29 years.

On the early morning of July 18, 1988, the "race" started.

The nerve-racking moment upon her child's birth was still fresh in Hongyan's memory: his whole body appeared purple, and his eyes were closed; the baby didn't cry nor make any movements. After being transferred to another hospital for rescue, an oxygen tube was inserted into one of his small nostrils, and a nasal feeding tube was inserted into the other; a nurse tried to give him an injection, but failed several times. Her sweat dropped onto the baby's wrinkled face, but he still had no reactions, not even raised his eyebrows.

"Severe cerebral palsy, and there's no point making more rescue efforts. Even if the baby is saved, he will become either paralyzed or mentally disabled in the future." After a while, the doctor came again and tried to persuade Zou, "Please think it over again for the baby and your own future. It's time to make a decision."

That night, Zou held her son in her arms without any sleep. The hot weather of the Jianghan Plain seemed to have no impact on the mother at all, as all her attention was on the baby's drooping eyelids, "This is mom, take a look at me!" "Since you've come to this beautiful world, why not open your eyes to see it …."

At five o'clock in the morning, the baby made a soft mutter like a kitten and finally gave out a cry. The doctor said that the cry meant the baby had been saved, but there must be a "long, painful, and arduous" life path awaiting him.

Zou gave her son the name "Ding Zheng," because she recalled the line "The trees are felled with the blows zheng-zheng, and the birds tweet ying-ying" in the *Book of Songs*, and hoped that he could at least leave some sounds in this world.

Keeping Ding Zheng alive was only the first step in their long journey ahead. How could she help him lead a better life? Zou set certain standards for that: having normal or almost normal body functions, mastering certain skills, developing a positive attitude toward life, and realizing and experiencing the fun and values of life.

The tests taken before Ding turned one year old showed that his intelligence was normal, but he was suffering from hemiparesis with difficulty moving his left foot. He always drooled, and his hands were too weak to hold anything. At the age of two and half, he learned to walk.

Zou led her son to various places for a cure. A doctor from the rare disease department of the Hubei University of Chinese Medicine told her that aged 3-6 was the golden period for a brain paralyzed child to receive massage treatment, but it required persistence as well as scientific trainings.

The boy had to have such treatment three times a week. Each time Zou would give him a bicycle ride after she had finished work. The road was bumpy. It was snowing heavily one day when their bike tipped over in a puddle and Ding rolled onto the ground. His mother helped him up, but the bike fell again. Zou put it in place, only to see her son had tumbled again .... Ding cried, and so did his mother.

The mother and son got to the hospital covered in mud. The doctor sighed, "I didn't think you would come because of the bad weather." "Even if it's raining knives, we will come for sure," Zou replied firmly.

The massage would last one hour each time. As the skin on his back was pinched up and twisted by the doctor's fingers, the three-year-old child often cried out in pain and gritted his teeth. He begged his mom several times not to go.

Zou was very clear that if they had missed one session, there would be a second time and even more .... "If I kept finding excuses, I would constantly forgive myself for not going," and the treatment could not be finished. She had to stay cool-headed and try her utmost to make a difference to the life of her son, a bit at a time.

The mother and son went through many hardships. Hope was like the morning sun that shone through dark clouds: first only a silver lining, then rays of sunshine escaped the clouds.

After he turned five years old, Ding Zheng could jump off the ground with both feet. That day, the boy spoke loudly to whoever he met in the yard, "See, I can jump, I can jump! Let me show you!" Her son's excited face was still fresh in Zou's memory.

During Ding's childhood, holding a pen and using chopsticks were both formidable tasks for him. Zou spent a whole year teaching her son the two skills. He is now grateful for her wisdom because if he hadn't mastered them, others might wonder why he can't use chopsticks at dinner. It saved them the trouble of having to explain his illness and thus avoid hurting his self-esteem.

However, the drawback of his body had made Ding attentive in whatever he was doing.

Before Grade 3, Ding wrote characters very slowly because of his awkward fingers. Zou asked the teacher to give her son some extra time to finish the exams. At first, he was allowed an additional 20 minutes, which was gradually reduced to five minutes. After Grade 4, the boy caught up with his classmates in writing speed and no more extra time was given to him.

"Mom has never tutored me in my homework," Ding said. When he had just entered primary school, she gave him a *Xinhua Dictionary*. Whenever the boy came across a new character, his mother would tell him, "Go look it up in the dictionary." In this way, Ding learned to study independently.

When Ding was in Grade 3, the teacher required the students' parents to design test papers for their children. After the students finished the test, their parents should check and mark it. Instead of doing so, Zou had been encouraging her son to make the exam questions and complete them all by himself. She always gave her son full marks without checking any of the answers.

One day, Ding returned home in low spirits. "Mom, you were criticized by our teacher today. Two of my answers were wrong, but you still gave me 100 points. She said you didn't shoulder your responsibility."

"I'll continue to give you 100 points in the future," Zou told her son calmly. "Since you designed the questions by yourself, it is unacceptable for you to make any mistakes when completing your test. You are slower than your classmates, so you should try to make it up by answering all the questions correctly."

Since then, Ding had formed the habit of checking each of his answers carefully, which led to an increase of accuracy. According to his mother, such habits prepared him to enter Peking University and Harvard University.

However, the great student also experienced setbacks.

Ding was recommended for admission to a key junior secondary school in Hubei Province. But only a few days after the term had begun, Zou, who was on a business trip, received a phone call from her son. "He was crying, saying that he didn't want to go to school anymore and asking me to return soon for the leaving procedures."

It turned out that when practicing leg lifts during a military training session, Ding along with some other students couldn't keep their balance.

All of them were criticized except Ding. When a few children complained about the unfair treatment they had received, the young instructor blurted, "He has brain paralysis." Someone thus mocked and played tricks on Ding and passed his pencil-box around away from him.

Zou set out that very night and hurried back to Wuhan after over 30 hours on a train. During the class break, she walked to the front of the classroom and said to the students, "Dear children, all of you are lucky to be healthy. But Ding Zheng is not. After growing up, you may become athletes, soldiers, pilots, or do whatever you like; but for him, there is no way out other than pursuing studies. Now he wants to quit school, so what could he do in the future? Will he be happy? Shouldn't we try to understand and tolerate him, and lend him a helping hand?" The whole class fell into silence.

During the end-of-term examination, Ding ranked at the top of his grade and had not been bullied ever again. After growing up, he recalled that experience, "Although Mom helped me out, I can't rely on her forever."

In Ding Zheng's mind, his mother has always been giving him guidance in a skilful manner. She often says, "Wisdom is required when it comes to educating children."

When Ding was in the second year of high school, he felt depressed due to his poor academic performance. He asked his mother, "Why should I work so hard to enter prestigious universities?"

Zou led her son to a building by East Lake. On the first floor, she asked him, "Can you see East Lake from here?"

"No, I can't."

After they ascended to the sixth floor, she asked again, "How about now?"

"I can see the lake now."

"Is it clear? Describe it to me."

"Not very clear. It looks just like a small handkerchief."

As they reached the 20th floor, they got a panoramic view of the vast lake.

"It is what East Lake truly looks like!" Mom told him that the lake was an objective reality, and the scene one could see depended on which platform he was standing on. Only by standing high could he see what he wanted.

Before long, Ding regained his top form. In 2007, he was enrolled by the College of Environmental Sciences and Engineering of Peking University with 660 points.

Years of rehabilitation training has helped improve Ding's condition significantly. He could basically live a normal life, except from doing precise actions such as using a thread and needle or conducting scientific experiments. In 2011, he transferred from his original major to international law and was then recommended for admission to the School of Transnational Law at Peking University as a postgraduate student.

Upon graduation, Ding worked in the legal department at a renowned internet company. After working there for one year, he felt an urge to further his studies. For the young man, Harvard University seemed to be "beyond his reach."

Zou was well aware of her son's level: He had been awarded a national scholarship twice, granted the title of "Three Goods Student of

Peking University," "Outstanding Graduate of Peking University" and "Outstanding Graduate of Beijing Municipality"; moreover, he had also achieved great academic results as a postgraduate student. After seeking advice from Ding's supervisor, she encouraged her son to give it a shot.

At first, Harvard rejected Ding. But after reading the reference letter from his supervisor, the university not only sent him an enrolment letter, but also exempted him from submitting the TOEFL test result.

Having successfully sent her son to Harvard after so many trials and tribulations, Zou doesn't think of herself as great. She'd rather define herself as "a mother who is making constant progress along with her child," and believes that she is not only her son's running partner during such a "marathon race," but also an athlete herself. The doctor's assertion made years ago that they would endure a "long, painful and arduous" life journey had become the source of strength and pleasure for her.

While raising her son, Zou has never slowed her pace in pursuing a better career: she is an associate professor, an up-and-coming teacher in Wuhan, Model Young Female Faculty of Wuhan, the First Batch of Outstanding Young Teachers of Wuhan, pacesetter of her field of study in the province, vice chairperson of the Association for Etiquette of Hubei Province, and a senior image adviser.

A painting has been hung on the wall of Zou's home for three decades: it depicts the scene of a winged little angel snuggling in her mother's arms. She bought the painting during her pregnancy. After discovering her baby's physical problems, she still regarded her son as the hope of the whole family, "Though with broken wings, he is still my angel …."

Ding Zheng repaid his mother's perseverance with action: he had never complained about wearing the old clothes given by others; to reduce traveling expenses, he only returned home during the summer and winter vacations; when studying as a postgraduate, he often walked to Tsinghua University under the scorching sun because the canteens there charged less.

Zou thinks that she and her son are just like the two strokes forming the character 人 (people), as they always support and accompany each other. Winning the fierce battle against death, breaking the assertion of "retarded or paralytic", entering Peking University and Harvard, all of these have been the milestones in their "life marathon", a journey that continues.

Ding's next goal is the upcoming Bar Examination. He studies 8 to 12 hours every day for it. "The test will be tough." He has some worries.

For Zou Hongyan, she hopes that she can offer some help to more children suffering from brain paralysis.

China currently has around six million brain paralysis patients, with the vast majority of them being children. Unfortunately, there is a lack of public awareness in the country concerning the illness and many people take it as mental maldevelopment. As a matter of fact, only less than 40% of brain paralytics have amentia. The prevalence and curability of the illness are not yet widely recognized. Many Chinese children are having no access to effective treatment, and some of them have died before reaching adulthood.

Having heard of Ding Zheng's success, many of Zou's friends introduced her to families with brain paralysis children. The mother and son thus decided to share their story with them in order to provide those with similar sufferings more encouragement and confidence.

Zou has set up a WeChat group in which people can talk with each other and exchange ideas about treatments. "Our persistence may help these children achieve self-reliance."

Ordinary People: Living a Vibrant Life
平凡老百姓：把日子过出精气神儿

宿管员霞姐的 N 个角色

The Multiple Roles of a Dormitory Supervisor

作者：雷 宇　刘明杨
翻译：薛彧威

宿管员霞姐的 N 个角色

在武昌理工学院的校园里,这个东四栋的宿管员——霞姐是女大学生们"火眼金睛"的保护神,也是没有代沟的最潮霞姐,有女生在她身上找到了"妈妈的味道"。她连续八个春节在学生宿舍度过。

李霞曾在武汉著名的电脑一条街广埠屯经营一家电子产品店。2009年,她追随做辅导员的丈夫来到该校,当了一名宿舍管理员。

每年9月,新生开始报到,入住宿舍。为了尽快熟悉学生,李霞会一个个做好信息登记,一有空儿就翻看新生住宿信息卡,晚上值班再专门到新生宿舍走访。楼栋里所有的进出登记、维修登记、重要事项通知等,在别人眼里是机械的重复工作,李霞却希望琢磨出一点儿不一样的东西。她最初的想法只是为了"不给当老师的丈夫丢脸"。

她给自己提了一个小要求:在最短的时

The Multiple Roles of a Dormitory Supervisor
宿管员霞姐的 N 个角色

间内记住每名学生的相貌、专业班级、寝室号及家庭住址。平时，李霞都会坐在公寓里看着走进走出的学生，从她们各自的特征去观察、判断，比如身高、体型、长相或者打扮，久而久之脑海里就会对她们形成一个大致的印象。她会时常主动去问同学们叫什么、家在哪里。特别是看到那些比较害羞、不爱说话的学生，她就喜欢把她们拉过来聊天，熟悉之后，同学们就会主动跟她打招呼。

渐渐地，李霞练成了一双"火眼金睛"。一栋宿舍楼700多人，她虽不能一一叫出名字，但都能认全，三分之一以上的同学可以道出姓名、专业甚至家庭情况，没有一个"不速之客"可以逃出她的"法眼"。"我眼睛小但聚光，只要我在门口坐着，就不可能有一个陌生人进去。"李霞笑着说，"女生宿舍必须绝对安全，我的职责是替她们的父母好好照顾她们。"

每天早晨6点多宿舍楼开门，是小偷小摸最容易混进宿舍的时候，李霞的"三板斧"屡试不爽。"你叫什么？哪个宿舍的？你的素质教育导师是谁？"三个问题一出，小偷没有不露馅儿的。有人冒充院系辅导员、学生会成员和社团成员混入新生宿舍实施诈骗，李霞制止预防的推销骗局就有20多起。学校宿管科每年开展"火眼金睛"宿管员认人大比拼，李霞年年得冠军，还都是满分。

除了做大学生安全的"保护神"，这个天生热心肠的宿管员还希望能成为孩子们的"知心人"。李霞深知，要想抓住青年学生的心，必须要积极学习，"跟上她们的步伐，会讲她们的语言"。看到不忙的同学，她总是主动请教，并学会了用QQ建群，学会了用微博、微信。她成为学校里第一个建楼栋QQ群、微信群的宿管员，通过这些平台，她可以及时发布通知、反馈情况、沟通信息，更好地为学生服务。李霞建的学生QQ群已有500多人加入，她的QQ好友里有近400人是宿舍学生及学生的父母。只要有空儿，李霞就主动和家长聊天，和他们一起交流学生成长。

由于和学生聊得来，不少学生还主动把她拉进班级QQ群，有了生活中的难题，同学们也总是去找"霞姐"倾诉。一次，一名学生身体不适在寝室哭，李霞知道情况后给学生冲红糖水，用热毛巾敷肚子，晚上给她煮面条，还送她去医院，让她感受到满满的温暖。护理学院的大二学生赵轩（化名）在她身上找到了"妈妈的味道"。刚入校时，赵轩慕名找到霞姐，说自己头总是特别痒。李霞让她到自己寝室坐下来，仔细查看，发现她头上有虱子。赵轩的妈妈已经去世了，她的爸爸还要带她妹妹，对她照顾没有那么细致。赵轩利用假期打工挣学费，虱子是因为打工的地方环境恶劣而染上的。听了赵轩的介绍，李霞的眼泪一下子就掉下来了。她一边安慰赵轩一边帮她喷药治疗。之后，李霞对赵轩更多了一份留意，专门帮她介绍了给小学生做家教的兼职。赵轩感冒了，李霞帮她煮生姜可乐；寒假里，赵轩兼职打工的地方不包住宿，李霞陪她住学校宿舍。

心细的霞姐还有"胆大"的传奇故事。2013年11月，一个周末的凌晨，平时睡眠就浅的李霞被楼上的声音惊醒，正疑惑间，一个女生推门喊她，声音急切而紧张。平日里，为了让学生随时能在最短的时间内找到自己，她所住寝室的门无论工作或休息都是虚掩着的。原来，一个陌生男子翻窗进入二楼一间宿舍阳台，击碎后门玻璃进入宿舍，向两名女生索要笔记本电脑和现金。其中一名女生趁男子不注意，跑出宿舍向李霞求救。李霞迅速披衣起身给保卫处打电话报警，并喊醒住在隔壁的宿管员。李霞拿起一根钢筋跑上楼，推开寝室门，对着盗贼大吼一声"干什么"，接着对宿舍内另一名女生喊"你出来"。那名女生一看霞姐来了，迅速跑出寝室。李霞看到盗贼惊慌迟疑，迅速将盗贼反锁在宿舍，随后与赶来的保卫处人员一起成功制服盗贼。整个事件前后不过5分钟。李霞事后回想起来，自己都有些后怕。

这个宿管员不仅管生活，还管思想。一天晚上，李霞正在吃饭，突然听到有学生说有人要跳楼，她放下饭碗，一边给学院领导打电话报告一边冲上楼去。学生看到她气喘吁吁地跑来，"哇"的一声哭了："霞姐，我失恋了，我不想活了！"李霞抱着学生，如同抱着自己的孩子，轻声安抚她。那天晚上，李霞和她的辅导员一起陪着她，听她诉说自己的恋爱经过，推心置腹地帮她寻求解决问题的方法，在这个过程中，学生的情绪也慢慢缓和下来。

"20岁的孩子就像花儿一样，他们有时候非常脆弱"，李霞说自己不会讲大道理，天气转凉时的一句叮嘱，考研前夜的一句鼓励，感冒时送上一碗姜汤，情感受挫时一个温暖的拥抱……她的陪伴无疑给了"花儿们"最大的安慰。还有一天傍晚，一个学生情绪不太好，单脚已跨到阳台外。李霞赶到宿舍时，学生已从阳台回到房间，房里只有她一人，正坐在椅子上发呆。经过一个多小时沟通，这名学生的脸色逐渐恢复正常。李霞害怕学生再次冲动，晚上就在这位女生的宿舍打了个地铺。第二天早上确定女生的情绪完全稳定之后，她又继续回去值班了。之后一段时间，李霞一直关注这名学生，"我要知道她吃好、睡好才能安心"。一个月后的一天，这名学生开开心心地来到值班室，说："阿姨，我以后遇见问题一定好好考虑，做个理智的成年人。"后来，她每每经过值班室，总是给李霞一个甜美的微笑。李霞说，这是一份发自内心的欣慰感，也是一种职业的幸福感。

李霞的声名早已超出了东四栋宿舍楼。另外一栋楼的大二姑娘张芳（化名）一度得了抑郁症，感觉朋友们都离自己远远的，这个世界都不像自己想象的样子。李霞注意到她的情况后，每次见面总是主动打招呼，慢慢约她到自己的值班室聊天。怎么交朋友，怎么看内心对朋友的猜疑，怎么安心学业，李霞不断释疑解惑，总是能说得小姑娘心悦诚服。

八年的寒假，李霞一直坚守在岗位。"节前有不少学生留校，有的要做兼职，有的准备复习考试，我得陪着她们"。除夕夜，留校学生基本都回家了，李霞一家在宿舍看着春晚过年。"学生都走了，可寝室里还有她们的电脑等贵重物品，这里一天24小时不能离人，每天都要巡楼几次。跟我对班的宿管阿姨要回老家过年，我就申请来值班。"李霞的家就在附近小区，但八年来，都是丈夫和女儿到学生宿舍来跟她团聚、陪她巡楼。

"付出的是爱心，收获的是亲情。"学生们都把霞姐当成知心朋友、可信赖的亲人，许多学生毕业后还与她保持联系：李霞的抽屉里珍藏着毕业生从全国各地寄来的明信片；很多孩子毕业后拿着第一个月的工资来请她吃饭；知道她长期留校过年，孩子们大年初三来给她拜年。2016年2月，这个普通的宿管员被评为学校"十佳管理工作者"，和一众教授一起获得了学校的奖励。"当时一个教授听说我是宿管员，连着向我们处长确认了三遍"。

"宿管员给人的印象就是大爷大妈，而李霞改变了人们对宿管员的认知，她自信、热情、乐观，与学生们打成一片。她不仅是生活的服务者，还是思想的引导者。"校领导在大会上评价她，浑身都是角色。

The Multiple Roles of a Dormitory Supervisor

Li Xia is a dormitory supervisor in charge of the East-4 residence hall on the campus of Wuchang University of Technology. To the female students she is Sister Xia, who is not only a guardian with piercing eyes, but also a fashionable older lady with no generation gap with them. Some even say they receive a kind of "motherly love" from her. During the Spring Festival holiday, when people normally go home, she stays in the dorm. She has done that for eight years now.

Li Xia used to run an electronics store at Guangbutun, a famous street in Wuhan where computerware is sold. In 2009 she followed her husband who came to the university for his new job as an instructor, and she found a job as a dorm supervisor.

Every September, new students report to the school and move into the dormitory. In order to quickly acquaint herself with them, she records their information one by one and flips through their pictures in the Fresh Students Dorm Cards in her spare time. During night shifts, she often visits their rooms. In the eyes of others, the job is very boring involving check-in information, maintenance records, and constant announcements. But Li Xia wanted to come up with something different. She was willing to try anything, with her only requirement that she not do anything that might bring embarrassment to her husband.

She set some rules for herself: try to remember every student's appearance, major, class, dorm number, and home address as quickly as she could. When sitting in the office, she would watch the students come and go, studying their features such as height, figure, appearance and style. Over time, a general impression would form in her mind. She would ask their names and hometowns. When meeting shy girls, she would initiate the conversations. But after a while, they would often be the first to talk to her.

As time went on, Li Xia developed "piercing eyes." Although she couldn't remember the names of all 700 plus students in the building, she could recognize their faces. She could recall the name, major, and even family background of over one third of the girls living there. No "uninvited guest" could escape her sharp eyes. "My eyes are small, but penetrating. As long as I sit at the entrance, not a single stranger can enter," Li said while smiling. "The girls' dormitory must be very safe, and it is my duty to take good care of them for their parents."

The dorm opens around 6 am, a time when thieves might sneak in. Li's "three questions" are an effective deterrent. "What's your name? Which room are you in? Who is your education advisor?" When asked these three questions, potential thieves reveal themselves. Some pose as teachers, student union representatives, or organization members to get into the dorms and defraud the new students. Li Xia has helped prevent more than 20 peddling frauds. In the annual "face recognition contest" held by the university's dormitory management section, Li always wins with full marks.

Aside from being the "protector" of the university students, the warm-hearted supervisor also hopes to become their friend. Li is keenly aware that in order to win the trust of the students, she should learn new things to "keep up with the times and speak their language." If a student is free, she'll ask questions on the latest topics. Already, she has learned how to set up QQ chat groups and can use microblogs and WeChat. She has become the university's first dorm supervisor to establish QQ and WeChat groups among the students living in the same building. Through these platforms, she can release notices, receive feedback and communicate with the students in a timely manner in order to provide them with better services. Their QQ group now has over 500 members, and nearly 400 of her QQ friends are those living in East-4 as well as their parents. When she has time, Li will chat with the parents about their children.

Many students have invited Li into their class QQ group. When running into a problem in life, they'll come to "Sister Xia" and tell her about it. One day, a girl didn't feel well and was crying in the dormitory. When she heard about this, Li gave her some brown sugar water and warmed her stomach with a towel. In the evening, she cooked noodles for the student and took her to the hospital. The student was deeply touched. Zhao Xuan (pseudonym), a sophomore student in the nursing college, is another student who found "motherly love" from Li. Zhao sought help from Sister Xia about her itchy scalp. Li invited the girl into her room to take a look. After a careful check, she found there were lice in her hair. Li discovered that Zhao's mom had passed away, and her dad had to raise her and her younger sister on his own, so he had little time to care for Zhao. The girl had to work part-time during vacations in a bad work environment, and this was where she got the lice. After hearing her story, Li Xia burst into tears. She tried to console the girl while spraying medicine in her hair. Since then, she has been paying special attention to Zhao and found another part-time job for her as a home tutor for elementary school students. When Zhao caught a cold, Li prepared some ginger cola for her. During winter vacations, Zhao's part-time job did not provide accommodation, so Li let Zhao stay with her at the school dormitory.

There is one particular story of Sister Xia's courage. On a weekend morning in November 2013, Li Xia, who was a light sleeper, was awakened by a sound upstairs. While trying to figure out what it was, a girl pushed her door open and cried out desperately. To make it easier for the students to reach her, Li often keeps her door unlocked, even if she is working or having a rest. The girl told Li that a stranger had climbed onto the balcony of the girl's second floor room. After smashing the glass, he broke into the room and intended to steal the laptops and cash from her and her roommate. The girl had escaped and came to Li for help. Li grabbed her clothes, made a phone call to campus security, and woke up another dorm supervisor sleeping next door. Then she picked up a steel bar and ran upstairs. She pushed the door open and shouted to the robber, "What are you doing here!" and said to the other girl, "Come out!" Seeing Sister Xia, the other girl ran out of the room immediately. The man panicked and hesitated, and Li locked him in. After the security guards arrived, Li helped them catch the robber. The entire incident lasted no more than five minutes, but the mere thought of it still scares her.

Sister Xia is not only in charge of the students' living situation, but also cares for their psychological well-being. One evening, Li was eating dinner when a student rushed over and said someone was trying to jump off the building. Li immediately dropped her bowl and called the college director to report the situation while dashing upstairs. Upon seeing Li out of breath, the girl burst into tears, "Sister Xia, I broke up with my boyfriend and don't want to live anymore!" Li was able to approach the girl and hug her while consoling her in a gentle voice, like a mother holding her child. That night, Li sat with the student and a teacher. They listened to her stories about what had happened between her and her boyfriend and tried to help her find a solution to the problem. The girl finally calmed down.

"20-year-olds are just like flowers; sometimes they can be very fragile." Li Xia says that because of their differences in age and experience, she can't talk about deep philosophies with the students, but she can instead offer them reminders when the weather turns cold, a word of encouragement on the eve of exams, a bowl of ginger soup when they catch colds, a warm hug when they experience bumps in their relationships .... To the "flowers," Sister Xia's company is a great comfort. One day at dusk, a student was depressed and nearly jumped off the balcony. When Li rushed over to her dormitory, the girl had returned to her room and was sitting alone in a daze. After a conversation for more than one hour with Sister Xia, her complexion gradually turned back to normal. Fearing that she might try to commit suicide again during the night, Li slept on a makeshift bed on the floor of her room. After making sure the girl's mood had stabilized the next morning, she went back to work again. Over the following days, she paid close attention to the student. "I could only feel relieved once I saw her eating and sleeping well." One month later, the girl came to Li's office joyfully and said to her, "Auntie, if I come across a problem again in the future, I will think it over carefully and try to be more rational." After this episode, whenever the girl passed by Li's window, she would give a sweet smile. According to Li, this was not only a sense of gratification, but also a feeling of happiness she had gained from her job.

Li's fame spread far beyond the East-4 Building. Zhang Fang (pseudonym), a sophomore girl living in another dormitory building, once suffered from depression. She felt that her friends were keeping a distance from her, and the world did no longer seem like what she had previously thought. After discovering this, Li would greet her each time they met and invite her for a chat in her office. They talked about many things, such as how to make friends, how to deal with one's suspicion towards a friend and how to dedicate oneself to studies. Sister Xia could always clear the girl's doubts away.

During winter vacations over the past eight years, Li Xia has stayed at her post. "Lots of students choose to stay at school until the Spring Festival. Some of them work part-time jobs while others make preparations for final exams. I choose to stay with them." By Spring Festival Eve, most students have left, and Li and her family celebrate by watching the Spring Festival Gala on TV in the dormitory. "Though the students are gone, their valuables are still here, such as their laptops. The building shall never be left unguarded, and we patrol it several times every day. A colleague of mine wanted to go home during the festival, so I stayed on duty." Li's home is nearby, but for eight consecutive years, her husband and daughter have joined her in the dormitory for Spring Festival and have accompanied her as she patrols the building.

"Li Xia has given her love and has received affection." The students all regard her as a close friend and even a trustworthy family member. Many of them still stay in touch with her after graduation. Her desk drawer is filled with postcards from students from various places across the country. Many students treat her to meals with their first monthly salary upon graduation, and some girls visit her during the Spring Festival on the third day of the first lunar month as they know she'll remain at her post during this period. In February 2016, she was conferred the title of "Top Ten Administrative Staff" by the university and received commendations along with several professors. "On hearing that I was just a dorm supervisor, one of the professors asked our section chief three times for confirmation," Li recalls.

During a recent conference, the university leadership praised her as "a person who has served multiple roles," saying, "In the eyes of many, dorm supervisors are usually those old uncles and aunties. Li Xia, however, has changed the stereotype with her confidence, passion, optimism, and her close friendship with the students. To them, she is not only a service provider, but also a mentor."

Scan for a Video

从震墟中起身，微笑向前

Rising from the Earthquake Ruins

作者：吴晓东
翻译：卢 敏

从震墟中起身,微笑向前

"好啊,打一局。"衡永红乐呵呵地接受了记者的"挑战"。

2018年5月,江风吹拂过露天球场,乒乓球飘忽不定地前蹿,27岁的衡永红穿着休闲T恤和牛仔裤,迎着风,专注而灵活地高推低挡。10年前,命运曾向她发了一个看上去不可抵挡的高难度球,但她顽强地"接球",将不可能变成了可能。当时,她是四川省北川中学高一（10）班的学生。在那次伤亡惨重的地震灾难中，她是一名幸运儿。

虽然命保住了，但她的腿几乎腐烂。衡永红已签字同意截肢，是重庆市急救中心的老专家们帮她一起打赢了这一回合，保住了双腿。尽管曾多次感受到"迎面跑来的死神所呼出的浊气"，但她没有沉沦在地震重伤的阴影里，而是开始新的人生航程，笑声清亮地行走在鲜花丛生的世界里。

灾难降临的前一天，地理老师正在为衡永红所在的北川中学高一（10）班讲地质知识，还提及到了地震话题。当晚，同学们还一起看了唐山大地震的图片和介绍。事实上，北川那段时间常常"地面发抖"，人们对地震并不陌生。

2008年5月12日，大地震来了。当时，衡永红和同学在上历史课，老师完成了讲解，学生正在自习。衡永红坐在第三排靠墙处，她感觉课桌开始剧烈且无规律地抖动。这时听到门外有人高喊"地震啦"！衡永红站了起来，地面摇得太厉害，师生们本能地往外跑。人流涌向后门逃生，门边就是楼梯。

她从第三排跑到倒数第二排时再也站不住，感觉楼板一下子倾斜，她摔倒在教室里的过道上。天花板坍塌下来，她眼前顿时一片漆黑。尘土和瓦砾掩盖住她的长发，呼吸时"感觉鼻孔全是灰尘，呛得睁不开眼睛"。她试图动一下身体，动弹不得。每过一会儿就有震动袭来，埋在废墟里的衡永红感觉"老是不停地在抖动"。黑暗中，她被恐怖的感觉重重包围。

事实上，她的教室位于5层教学楼的第三层，下面的两层楼已经沉降到地面以下，她所在的楼面被推到一个角落。意识到自己还活着的时候，衡永红有惊喜、庆幸，也有慌乱、不知所措。她发现自己被压住了。镇定下来后，她发现左手能稍微转动，于是小心地挤开碎砖，左手终于能活动了。这给了绝望中的她一丝希望，她用左手先后"解放"了右手、头部和上半身。整个过程非常艰难，但她有了更大的空间呼吸，上身能够微微弯曲，"感觉好受多了"。周围伸手不见五指。她用手摸索着，发现大腿上压着横梁，很重，怎么掀都纹丝不动，在横梁上方还压着预制

Rising from the Earthquake Ruins
从震墟中起身，微笑向前

板。重压下的大腿最初钻心地疼，后来不觉得疼了，却胀得厉害，很难受。她把手穿过横梁旁的微小缝隙，尽力清理小腿附近的废墟。等小腿能微微动弹时，她缩回手，发现全是血，手都是湿的。她一直在出汗，衣服完全湿透，等她确认无法清理更多时，她沮丧地发现，腿已经肿得极其严重。她的小腿前端和脚部位置压着另一个同学，最初那个同学还有温度，后来慢慢地变凉了，她明白发生了什么，但这反而激发了她的求生欲，"必须坚持下去"！

周围渐渐传来各种声音，夹杂着呻吟、呼救、哭泣。衡永红确认有同学活着，"感觉他们的状态还可以。"她听到了邻座侯天凤的声音，她说腿也被压住了；女生苏阳的声音比较微弱，感觉状态不太好；男生付敏表示被困在一张桌子下；稍远处还传来男生景垚垚的声音。"我们相互鼓励，说一定努力坚持，要活下去"。他们用有人在地下过了七天七夜的故事彼此激励，提醒每过几分钟就相互叫一下。大家在废墟里讲述"出去以后想干什么"，讨论怎样才能尽快自救。

在漆黑一片的废墟里，衡永红想到了自己的梦想，"我还有那么多事要做，不能就这么死了"。父母关爱自己的细节像电影一样从衡永红眼前一幕幕闪过。"我要考大学，找一份好的工作，报答他们，不能就这样死了。如果我死了，他们怎么办？爸妈对我那么好，怎么能接受？"

她一直坚持，不敢睡觉，害怕一睡过去就再也醒不过来。事实上，救援一直在继续。废墟下的几个人一起呼救，吸引了几名师生的注意，当天，苏阳等四人获救。救援者掏出一个洞口，废墟深处的衡永红看见了光，看见了天上的月亮，还看见点点星星仿佛在对自己眨眼，"在那一刻，我懂得了生命、光亮的含义"。

她借着月光审视自己的处境，假如往前或往后一点儿，都会被坚硬的砖头和预制板砸中，必死无疑，而她待在一个墙角的小缺口处，幸运地避开了死神。外面的人看见了衡永红，接力救援开始了。可是，她大腿上的横梁无法撼动。一拨儿高三同学冒着余震的危险爬进洞口，帮衡永红把空间尽量扩大一些，一名男生摸遍口袋，把仅剩的一块牛奶片给了她。

天色渐晚，同学们没有离去，在洞口围成一圈，唱起当时很流行的歌曲，"每一次／就算很受伤也不闪泪光／我知道／我一直有双隐形的翅膀／带我飞／飞过绝望……"歌声鼓励她坚持下去。深夜里，一名高三男生不顾危险跳进洞口，给她一盒牛奶和一块巧克力。他背靠背抵着衡永红，"你不要说话，过段时间就应我一声，不要睡过去。"夜深了，气温转凉，他又去找了一件厚厚的牛仔服给她披上。

这是一个漫长的夜晚。衡永红每次睁开眼睛都发现月亮还在原处，夜空一点点暗下去，但感动和希望却一点点在心里升起来。她极度困乏，但不敢睡觉，只能闭目养神。每当听见一点声音，她就感受到生的可能，不由自主地睁开眼。腿部的肿胀感让她异常难受，"也许我的腿保不住了"，这个爱美的高中女生开始了各种想象和权衡。

天亮了，又一支救援队赶到。几个人轮流进入洞口，将衡永红身下的地板敲出一个洞，逐渐凿大，小心翼翼地将压在她身上的横梁敲掉部分。努力有进展，但没有改变根本格局。衡永红希望能直接把自己"拔"出来。

"把你腿拔断了怎么办？""如果为了这条腿，人死掉，不划算。我宁可断腿，求你们把我拔出去。"

一场充满了信任、友爱、担心和希冀的揪心救援开始了。在废墟下的洞口，素不相识的救援者抱住17岁的女生，摸索着往外拔。左脚相对轻松地拔了出来，可她肿得异常厉害的右腿没法拉动。救援者伸手去探时，发现手套上全是血。没人敢拉了。"腿会断的！"衡永红表现出与年龄不相称的理性，重申"腿拉断了，我不会怪你，只会感谢你"。她的腿几无知觉，她已准备一辈子坐在轮椅上，"但是我要活着"。

她被小心翼翼地拉出来了，腿鲜血淋漓，呈暗紫色，全是挤压形成的撕裂伤口。因为又一条生命被救出，洞口传来欢呼，衡永红参与其中——她为自己庆幸，更为救援中得到的关爱而深深感动。一群素昧平生的人为了生命的顽强，为了生的信念，满含热泪地抱在一起。

衡永红伤情太重，被转送到绵阳中心医院。一名志愿者为她拿来一包小面包，她完全吃不下，把面包放在头下枕着，非常疲惫的她感觉很舒服，随后陷入意识模糊。她在半梦半醒中接受了减压手术。因为没有麻药，有人给了她一瓶七喜，她咬住瓶盖，手术做完时，瓶盖已被咬得面目全非。

她腿上最大最长的伤口深可见骨，令人不忍直视，从几处伤口渗出的血液浸透了被子。她的脸色白得像纸一样。死神又一次向她走来。她昏迷过去，一天后才醒来。她看见身旁挂着的液体和血液，听见一些年长医生的声音，询问她是否愿意到医疗条件更好的重庆去医治。

她表示同意。没法找到家属签字，衡永红签下了自己的名字，"如果有什么情况，我自己可以负责"。救护车即将开动时，她的爸爸和二叔气喘吁吁地赶到了。原来，她的家乡坝底乡也受灾严重，乡民们通过电视了解灾情和救援情况。她的父亲衡世森决定

"就算丢命也要去找女儿"。

由于道路和山体受损严重，衡世森和二弟翻了十多座山，一刻不停地走了一天，才走到北川县城。这位中年男人坚持要找到女儿，哪怕找到的只是遗体。寻亲的信息在人群中传递。衡永红的同学将她的信息告诉了自己的舅舅，这位热心的舅舅恰好认识衡世森，他骑着摩托车到处找，终于把忧心忡忡的父亲接到女儿的救护车旁。

这是一个残酷又温情的时刻，经历生离死别的父女俩抱头痛哭。父亲欣喜若狂，可看到女儿伤情如此严重，又背过身去伤心抽泣。人生的悲欢在这一刻达到极致。她的父亲陪她去重庆，而二叔则步行回家传递她还活着的好消息，"她人还活着，但腿可能保不住了，颜色都发紫了"。

幸运的是，衡永红遇见了一群医者仁心的老专家，他们延续了女孩瑰丽的梦。2008年5月18日凌晨2时，衡永红被重庆市急救医疗中心的120救护车接至重庆。当日14时左右，急救医疗中心的创伤科、骨科、麻醉科专家联合为她手术。做完手术，所有医生都留下来等她自然醒。

手术很成功！腿也有可能保住！这超乎期待。在绵阳时，她本人已经签字同意做截肢手术了。衡永红并不知道，因为自己的伤情过于严重，已经出现了急性坏疽症，是否要保住腿，医生是有分歧的，业界名声显赫的大专家为此冒了"或许把自己的名气砸进去"的风险。

在医生名声和年轻人未来生活质量之间，专家们做了最有利于患者的选择。手术前，主治医生告诉衡永红手术的风险及保肢的难度，"尽管有困难，但我们愿意努力尝试一下，你要有心理准备，更要有决心。奇迹很难，但试试或许有奇迹；你心里一定不要放弃，我们一起努力！"清创减压手术完成后，经过一周观察、换药，她左脚足背血流恢复、脚趾活动逐渐正常；再往后，右腿也开始长出肌肉，双腿都保住了。

在重庆急救中心救治期间，两名志愿者每天到病房为她补课：西南政法大学的研究生胡金星为她补理科，西南大学的牛静雯为她补文科。这让她没有落下太多功课。

在治疗期间，衡永红得到了医护人员无

微不至的关心和照顾。地震的伤痛慢慢被抚平，她就像一个大家庭里辈分最小、最受宠爱的孩子。出院时，她已经把这里当成第二个家。初回北川，她需要拐杖，没法维持身体平衡，但她顽强地进行康复训练。秋季开学后，她半天在学校半天在医院，坚持读书。

在"帐篷中学"，以此前的10班学生为主，组成了新的班级。新班主任陈丹建议她留级，但她坚持随班就读。毕业时，把重庆当作了第二故乡的她，选择报考长江师范学院，学习财务管理。她没有辜负人们的期望，顺利考取会计证书，每年拿奖学金，入党，在学校表现优异。

毕业后，她通过公开考试，如愿以偿进入重庆急救医疗中心，在财务科工作，"我终于通过努力奋斗，回到了第二个家！"岁月慢慢抹平了地震带来的不适、痛苦和伤害，这个年轻女孩的生命再次如鲜花般盛开。

如今，她参加工作已有四年多。除了认真工作，她也非常投入地享受人生。"闻一阵花香、烫一片毛肚、唱一首老歌，都让我感受到生命的快乐。在废墟里的时候我就想，要是能活下来，我一定要好好活着，我要履行对自己的承诺。"她说，乐观的心态是战胜心理阴霾最可靠的武器。

如今，衡永红并不忌讳谈论地震，她能平静地复述自己地震时的经历，不介意让外人看到伤疤，但她不会絮絮叨叨就这事烦个没完。她会和同学们一起为地震中罹难的同学送花祈福，有时也会折千纸鹤或写一些文字纪念他们，并和所有豆蔻年华的少女一样，期待一场轰轰烈烈的美好爱情。

Rising from the Earthquake Ruins

"Okay, game on." Heng Yonghong cheerfully accepted the journalist's "challenge."

In May 2018, the river breeze blew across the open-air court as the table tennis ball bounced forward. Facing the wind, 27-year-old Heng Yonghong wore a casual T-shirt and jeans and played attentively and flexibly. Ten years ago, destiny served her a difficult ball that seemed hard to defend, but she tenaciously "hit the ball back" and made the impossible possible. At that time, she was a student of Class 10, Grade 1 of Beichuan High School in Sichuan Province. She was a lucky girl in the earthquake that claimed many lives.

Although her life was spared, her legs were almost lost. Heng Yonghong signed a medical agreement on amputation. It was the senior experts in Chongqing Emergency Center who helped save her legs. She was threatened by death several times, but she did not sink into the shadow of the severe injury from the earthquake. She embarked on a new life journey, walking in a world full of flowers with clear laughter.

The day before the disaster struck, a geography teacher was teaching geology to the students in Class 10, Grade 1 of Beichuan High School. The teacher spoke about earthquakes. That evening, the students saw the pictures of and introduction to the Tangshan earthquake. The land of Beichuan often shook during that time, and people knew one thing or two about earthquakes.

On May 12, 2008, a powerful earthquake struck. At that time, Heng Yonghong and her classmates were taking a history class, the teacher finished lecturing, and the students were studying independently. Heng Yonghong was sitting in the third row against the wall, and she felt that her desk began to shake violently and irregularly. At that time, someone out of doors shouted "Earthquake!" Heng Yonghong stood up, the ground shook fiercely, and the students and teachers instinctively ran out. People flocked to the back door to escape as there were stairs next to the door. When she ran from the third row to almost the last row, she could no longer stand, feeling that the floor suddenly tilted, and she fell onto the aisle in the classroom. The ceiling collapsed, and the world became dark. Dust and rubble covered her long hair, and when she breathed, she felt that her nostrils were full of dust, and she couldn't open her eyes. She tried to move her body, but she couldn't. Shocks continued wave upon wave. Heng Yonghong, who was buried in the earthquake ruins, felt that she was constantly shaking. In the darkness, she sank into horror.

Her classroom was located on the third floor of a five-story teaching building. The two floors below had sunk into the ground, and the floor she was on had been pushed to a corner. When she realized that she was still alive, Heng Yonghong felt surprisingly lucky, and also helpless. She found herself stuck in rubble. After calming down, she noticed that her left hand could turn slightly, so she carefully pushed away the broken bricks, and her hand was finally able to move. This gave her a glimmer of hope in despair. She used her left hand to free her right hand, head, and upper body.

The whole process was very difficult, but she had more space to breathe, and her upper body was able to bend slightly, making her "feel much better." She couldn't see anything around her. She fumbled around with her hands and found that a beam was on her thighs. It was so heavy that she couldn't move it no matter how hard she tried, and the precast slab was on the beam. Under heavy pressure, her thighs acutely ached at first, but after some time, she no longer felt any pain, only the discomfort caused by her swollen legs. She stretched her hands into the tiny gaps beside the beam and tried her best to remove the rubble near her shins. When her shins could move around slightly, she retracted her hands and found that they were covered with blood. She was sweating the entire time, and her clothes were drenched. When she was convinced that she couldn't remove any more rubble, she found that her legs were extremely swollen. Near her feet was a classmate. At first, the classmate felt warm, and then slowly became cold. She understood what was happening, but this only made her desire to survive stronger. She said to herself, "I must survive."

Various sounds gradually came from around her, mixed with groans, cries for help, and weeping. Heng Yonghong was convinced that some of her classmates were alive. She said, "They sounded okay." She heard the voice of Hou Tianfeng, who sat next to her in class and said that her legs were also stuck in rubble; the voice of Su Yang, a schoolgirl, who was weak and not in good condition. Fu Min, a schoolboy, said that he was trapped under a desk; the voice of Jing Yaoyao, a schoolboy, was heard a little farther away. "We encouraged one another and said that we must hang in there and survive." They motivated one another with stories about someone who spent seven days below ground. They did a roll call every few minutes. In the earthquake ruins, they talked about what they wanted to do after getting out and discussed how to save themselves as soon as possible.

In the darkness under the earthquake ruins, Heng Yonghong thought of her dream. "I still have many things to do. I can't die." Her parents' care for her flashed in her mind like movies. "I want to be admitted to a university, find a good job, and repay them, so I can't die. If I die, how will they carry on with their lives? My parents are so kind to me. How can they accept my death?"

She did not dare to sleep. She was afraid that she would never wake up if she did. The rescue continued. Several people under the rubble called for help together, which drew the attention of several teachers and students. On the same day, Su Yang and three other students were rescued. The rescuers dug a hole, and Heng Yonghong, in the depths of the earthquake ruins, saw the light and the moon in the sky as well as the stars as if they were blinking at her. "At that moment, I understood the meaning of life and light."

In the moonlight, she assessed her situation. If she had moved forward or backward, she would have been hit by bricks and a precast slab. She would surely have been killed. She stayed in a small gap in the corner and fortunately escaped death. People saw Heng Yonghong, and they began to rescue her. However, the beam on her thigh could not be lifted. A group of senior secondary school students of Grade 3 climbed into the hole at the risk of aftershocks to help Heng Yonghong expand the space as much as possible. A schoolboy reached into his pockets and gave her the only milk candy he had.

It was getting late, but the students did not leave. They formed a circle around the entrance of the hole and sang a popular song, "When I am hurt every time, I don't shed a tear. I know I always have a pair of invisible wings, which accompany me to fly over despair ...." The singing encouraged her. Late at night, a third-grade schoolboy in a high school jumped into the hole regardless of danger and gave her a box of milk and a piece of chocolate. He leaned against Heng Yonghong, saying, "Don't speak, but please answer my call from time to time. Don't fall asleep." Late at night, the temperature dropped, and he went to find a thick denim jacket to wrap around her.

This was a long night. Every time Heng Yonghong opened her eyes, she found that the moon was still there, and the night sky darkened, but she was moved and hopeful in her heart. She was extremely sleepy but did not dare to sleep, so she could only close her eyes and rest. Whenever she heard a sound, she felt the possibility of life and opened her eyes instinctively. The swelling of her legs made her extremely uncomfortable. She thought, "Maybe I'll lose my legs." This senior secondary schoolgirl, who loves beauty, began to imagine and consider all things.

At dawn, another rescue team arrived. Several people took turns to enter the hole, breaking a hole on the floor under Heng Yonghong's body, gradually expanding it, and carefully knocking off a part of the beam that was pressed on her body. They were making progress but still could not help her out safely. Heng Yonghong hoped to be pulled out.

"What if your legs are broken?" "If I die for my legs, it's not worthwhile. I'd rather break my legs. Please pull me out."

A rescue full of trust, love, anxiety, and hope began. At the opening in the earthquake ruins, a rescuer carried the 17-year-old schoolgirl in his arms and tried to lift her. Her left leg was pulled out relatively quickly, but her abnormally swollen right leg could not be pulled out. The rescuer extended his hands to reach for the leg. When he withdrew his hands, he found that the gloves were covered with blood. No one dared to pull it. "Her right leg will be broken!" Heng Yonghong appeared more rational than her peers and reiterated that "If my right leg is broken, I will not blame you. I will only thank you." Her legs were numb, and she was prepared to sit in a wheelchair for the rest of her life. "I want to survive."

She was carefully pulled out, and her legs were dark purple and dripping with blood, with lacerations formed by squeezing and pressing. Because another life had been rescued, people cheered. Heng Yonghong felt fortunate and was deeply moved. For the tenacity of life and the belief in survival, a group of people who did not know one another hugged each other with tears in their eyes.

Heng Yonghong was seriously injured and was taken to Mianyang Central Hospital. A volunteer brought her a packet of bread. She couldn't eat it at all. She put the bread under her head. She was exhausted but felt very comfortable, and then she was in a coma. She got decompression surgery when she was barely conscious. Because there was no anesthetic, someone gave her a bottle of 7UP. She bit the bottle cap. When the operation was completed, the bottle cap was deformed.

The bone from the biggest and longest wound on her leg was visible, and many people could not bear to see it. The blood from several wounds soaked the quilt. Her face was as white as paper. She faced death again. She was in a coma and woke up a day later. She heard the voice of an elderly doctor asking if she would like to go to Chongqing for better medical treatment conditions.

She agreed. Unable to find her family members to sign a medical agreement, Heng Yonghong signed her name on it herself, "If anything happens to me, I can be responsible for it myself." When the ambulance was about to set off, her father and uncle arrived in exhaustion. It turned out that her hometown, Badi Township, was also seriously affected. The villagers learned about the disaster and the relief efforts from the TV. Her father, Heng Shisen, decided to find his daughter at the risk of his own life.

Due to severe damages to the roads and mountains, Heng Shisen and his brother climbed over a dozen mountains. They kept walking for a day before they reached Beichuan County. The middle-aged man persisted in finding his daughter, alive or dead. The messages of looking for relatives were circulated among the people. Heng Yonghong's classmate told his uncle about her. The warm-hearted uncle happened to know Heng Shisen. He rode a motorcycle to look for him and finally took her worried father to his daughter's ambulance.

This was a cruel and affectionate moment. The father and daughter who had experienced life and death cried in each other's arms. The father was thrilled, but when he realized his daughter's wounds were so serious, he turned his back and sobbed sadly. At this moment, the joys and sorrows of life went to extremes. Her father accompanied her to Chongqing, while her uncle walked home to deliver the good news that she was still alive. "She is still alive, but her legs have turned purple and may be lost."

Fortunately, Heng Yonghong met a group of senior experts who were as kind as they were skillful, and they helped the girl attain her dream. At 2 a.m. on May 18, 2008, Heng Yonghong was picked up by the 120 Ambulance of Chongqing Emergency Medical Center to Chongqing. At around 2 p.m. that day, the trauma, orthopedics, and anesthesiology specialists of Chongqing Emergency Medical Center jointly operated on her. After the operation, all the doctors stayed and waited for her to wake up.

The operation was a success and she was able to retain her legs. This was beyond her expectation. When she was in Mianyang, she signed a medical agreement on amputation operations. At that time, Heng Yonghong didn't know that because her wounds were so serious that she had already suffered from acute gangrene. Doctors were split on whether to keep her legs. Well-known medical experts took the risk of "perhaps tarnishing their reputations."

Between their reputation and the life quality of the girl, the experts made the choice that was most beneficial to the patient. Before the operation, the attending doctors told Heng Yonghong about the risks of surgery and the difficulty in saving her legs. "Although there are difficulties, we are willing to try our best. You must be mentally prepared and determined. It is hard to work a miracle, but we may try for it. Be hopeful, and let's work hard together!" After the debridement and decompression surgery, through a week of observation and dressing, the blood flow on the dorsum of her left foot was restored, and the movement of her toes gradually became normal. Later, the muscle on the right leg began to grow. Both of her legs were saved.

During the treatment at Chongqing Emergency Medical Center, two volunteers went to her ward every day to help her make up lessons: Hu Jinxing, a postgraduate of Southwest University of Political Science & Law, helped her with science subjects, and Niu Jingwen from Southwest University taught her liberal arts subjects. This kept her from missing too many lessons.

During her treatment, Heng Yonghong received the meticulous care of the medical staff. Her injuries slowly healed, and she was like the youngest and most beloved child in a big family. When she was discharged from the hospital, she had already regarded it as her second home. When she went back to Beichuan, she needed crutches and couldn't maintain the balance of her body, but she was tenaciously engaged in rehabilitation training. After the school started in fall, she spent half a day at school and half a day in the hospital and persisted in studying.

In the "Tent High School," a new class mainly consisting of the former students of Class 10 was formed. The homeroom teacher of the new class, Chen Dan, advised her to repeat the grade, but she insisted on attending the same class. When she graduated, she regarded Chongqing as her second hometown and chose to apply to Yangtze

Normal University to study financial management. She lived the good life as people had wished for her: she passed the accounting certificate exam, got a scholarship every year, became a Party member, and performed well at university.

Upon graduation, she passed the examination and fulfilled her wish to work in the Finance Section of Chongqing Emergency Medical Center. "I have finally returned to my second home through my hard study!" The years slowly removed the trauma, pain, and injury caused by the earthquake. The life of this young girl bloomed like flowers again.

To date, she has been working for more than four years. In addition to working hard, she also enjoys life enthusiastically. "Smelling the fragrance of flowers, dip-boiling a slice of tripe, and singing an old song all made me feel the joy of life. When I was trapped in the earthquake ruins, I thought if I could survive, I must live a better life, and I must keep that promise." She said that an optimistic attitude was the most reliable weapon to overcome the trauma.

Now Heng Yonghong does not refrain from talking about the earthquake. She can calmly retell her experience during the earthquake. She doesn't mind letting other people see her scars. She and her classmates send flowers and blessings to those who died in the earthquake and sometimes fold paper cranes or write some words to commemorate them. Like all the young girls, she hopes for passionate and beautiful love.

Scan for a Video

满地六便士，他抬头看见月亮

Sixpence Is Everywhere, But He Looks Up and Sees the Moon

作者：朱娟娟
翻译：卢　敏

满地六便士，他抬头看见月亮

"交出好吃的！"一名"劫匪"手拿"匕首"，步步逼近一名小学生。这名小学生瞅了瞅怀里的一包方便面，几乎没有一点犹豫，朝相反的方向抛去，继而脱身。

台下学生笑得前俯后仰，同时为台上学生的冷静机智拍手叫好。

这一幕，发生在湖北省恩施土家族苗族自治州巴东县白沙坪小学六年级的课堂上。

这是一堂生命安全教育课。窗外是连绵的大山，教室里，墙上绿色的油漆剥落斑驳，水泥地面坑坑洼洼。教师袁辉没有照本宣科，而是将知识点设计成一个个类似的情景剧。学生们随时上台"出演"角色，袁辉不时穿插提问。

这样融合情景剧的教学，在袁辉的课堂上很常见。

袁辉毕业于南京大学历史系，大学时喜欢研究国际政治。2012年毕业后，他来到距离家乡 1000 多公里的乡村小学支教，至今已是第六年。课下，孩子们喜欢喊他"袁哥"。

"袁哥"面容平和、阳光。30 岁了，他没买房买车，也没恋爱结婚。与许多年轻人一样，在大学毕业的关口，袁辉也面临过选择。

毕业前夕，导师写了封亲笔信，推荐他到南京市一家杂志社工作。面试后，总编辑对他很满意。回去的路上，袁辉犹豫了。他想起高中时的梦想。那时，看到一些学校填鸭式的教学模式下学生成为"考试机器"，袁辉就想，有没有其他方式，学生既能真正掌握知识，又能快乐学习与成长？他希望自己能为教育领域的发展注入新的力量。在高中，他碰到过的好老师既才华横溢又平易近人，有时在校园里遇到，他会冲过去一把抱住老师。他觉得，教师这个职业挺好。

相比城市的车水马龙、嘈杂熙攘，袁辉更喜欢农村。小时候，他曾在农村生活过一段时间，那里蓝天白云，绿树成荫，捉泥鳅、钓龙虾都成为美好的回忆。去农村支教的想法在他心中越来越清晰。最终，他婉谢了老师与杂志社的好意，背起行囊，向西出发了。

袁辉先后去过四川省马边彝族自治县、贵州都匀县的两所学校，不凑巧，两校暂时不缺教师。他想起在电视上看过湖北省巴东县"拐杖教师"谭定才坚守乡村教学点的事迹，于是他坐上火车转汽车再转三轮车，来到谭老师所在的清太坪镇姜家湾教学点。

眼前的小伙子让谭定才有些疑虑：一个名牌大学生，千里迢迢来山里的教学点教书，想清楚了吗？谭定才劝导他再考虑考虑，回去找份好工作。袁辉很坚定。清太坪满目葱翠、山野清新，孩子们纯净清澈的眼神更让他确信这里就是自己想要待的地方。报当地教育部门备案同意后，他找了间空教室，安置了下来。

支教生活并不轻松。

课堂上，孩子们一个比一个拘谨；课下，有的调皮捣蛋。袁辉一点点找原因，这里是国家级贫困县，孩子们有的是留守儿童，有的来自单亲家庭。

"越是这种情况，越要保护孩子们的天

性，玩时放得开、打开心扉，学习时也要静得下心来、提高效率，做到既长本领又快乐阳光，能收能放。"袁辉边琢磨边摸索，很快设计出融合情景剧元素的课堂教学模式。

在讲好书本知识的基础上，袁辉尽量让孩子们接触和大城市一样的素质教育。他曾开了一门"古典文化课"，教古诗与古汉语。讲贾岛的《剑客》时，袁辉找来墨镜与玩具剑当道具，与学生们比表演，表情、身姿、吟诗……看谁更有剑客风范。

他还带领大家一起写现代诗、打油诗、镜像字、画画。优秀作品由孩子们来评定，然后贴在教室墙上。

渐渐地，附近学校同行都知道了，姜家湾教学点来了个袁老师，教课很有新意。2014年，同一个乡镇的白沙坪小学缺乏年轻教师，校长找到袁辉，请他过去工作。

白沙坪小学有6个年级，共85名学生。袁辉担任六年级班主任，同时教五、六年级的数学课、思想品德课，以及三、四年级的音乐课。他每周在校上31节课，教学量几乎是其他老师的两倍。

最近，巴东县全县4700多名六年级学生统一参加期中考试，袁辉带的班级有三分之一的学生数学成绩进入全县前1000名。

每天在校内上6节课，校外，袁辉还带了个"一个人的课堂"。

今年12岁的青青（化名）是白沙坪小学五年级在籍学生。由于从小习惯性骨折，青青一年级时没在学校待几个月就只得回家，整天坐在轮椅上。不忍看到青青辍学，袁辉每周到青青家义务上课，每周去两到三次，每次往返20公里。山路坑洼，风吹雨打，"一个人的课堂"持续至今，袁辉骑坏了两辆摩托车。青青每次考试成绩排名，几乎都在班级前列。袁辉不仅分文不取，还常常给青青带去字典、书籍、牛奶等。受袁辉影响，青青的姐姐考上了师范生，打算大学毕业后也当一名教师。青青一家对袁辉满是感激。但袁辉把自己的付出看得很淡。在他看来，轮椅上的青青不仅坚强，还喜欢学习，也带给他积极的影响。

学生小勇（化名）的妈妈离家出走，爸爸瘫痪在床。看到父子俩生活不方便，袁辉买了箱方便面送去。过了一阵子，袁辉问小勇方便面吃完没，小勇说舍不得吃，准备留到过年时吃。这让袁辉很感慨，生活这么困难，但在孩子脸上看不到一丝悲伤。随后，他又买了些米、面送过去，看到父子俩的床单又脏又旧，袁辉买来新的，帮忙换上。网友及袁辉的大学同学、华中农业大学的大学生志愿者一起凑了些钱。现在，小勇家新添了电视机，生活也有所改善。

青青、小勇等学生的故事，被袁辉发到微信朋友圈上。从2016年起，华中农业大学、中南民族大学、中南财经政法大学、南京大学的大学生志愿者们，陆续来到白沙坪小学，与学生结对帮扶，或是暑期来校参与支教。

支教6年了，袁辉把自己定位为一名志愿者。这也意味着他收入不高，每月仅1000余元，是其他在编教师的四分之一。相比收入，他更看重自由与自在。每天可以读喜欢的书、呼吸新鲜空气、每周都去爬山……袁辉觉得，这样的乡村生活简单却丰富；同时，孩子们也是他的朋友，"我可能带给他们不一样的视角,但他们也带给我欢乐与陪伴。如果没有他们,日子肯定也单调。"

十几平方米的宿舍里,袁辉摆了5张书桌,堆满了哲学、历史、文学等各类书籍,还珍藏着一届届学生送给他的礼物。一个专门的储物箱内,最多的是学生手工做的贺卡,还有竹制的笔筒。一名学生送他用纸包好的棒棒糖,袁辉也舍不得吃。这些贺卡上,有的贴着孩子们亲手采摘、风干的花朵,有的画着各种小动物。笔筒上,刻着花花草草,写着祝福的话语。

山里孩子特有的淳朴,让袁辉收获了不一样的记忆。

一次,袁辉骑车摔倒在地,一侧胳膊与脸上擦破了皮。几个学生知道后,凑零花钱买了棉签和碘酒,结伴来看老师。他们排着队,有的拿棉签,有的擦碘酒,还问他疼不疼。还有的把平时舍不得吃的八宝粥也拿了过来。

支教的生活一贯清苦。在姜家湾教学点时,袁辉的父亲从徐州来探望,看到他"家徒四壁",住处连自来水都没有,洗衣服靠接雨水，顺着瓦檐流下的雨水放久了，表面都有黑色的游虫，吃水、做饭得去对面山头提山泉水……联想到其他同事亲朋的孩子，大学毕业后纷纷留在大城市成家立业，父亲再也忍不住，与袁辉争了起来。袁辉还是没走。他已经想好了，每个人有每个人的活法，这里需要他，他在这里有自己的收获，想要继续待下去。

第二天，劝说无果的父亲独自踏上回家的路，路上发来短信说"儿子，对不起"。想到不能照料父母，袁辉也回复"对不起，爸爸"。父亲回去不久，家里给他寄来一件厚实的大衣。那之后，父母再没有劝他离开。

作为一个现代青年，袁辉没有个人电脑，他觉得不需要，办公室有台式机可以用。网购基本局限于买书。他最爱的书是尼采的《查拉图斯特拉如是说》，一共有7个译本，他每天都读。

袁辉一直与外界保持着较为密切的联系。他的中学、大学同学来看他，但常常是同学请他吃饭。这些同学还带来善款，捐给有需要的孩子。共青团湖北省委、团恩施州委、巴东县委等也长期关注着袁辉,给袁辉所在的白沙坪小学的孩子们送来爱心物资。

他也不爱出去旅游,但每周必定要去周围爬一座山。他的微信朋友圈里,出现最多的是孩子们的笑脸;其次是巴东的美景,青山巍峨,白云飘飘;再然后是他自己写的古体诗。

2016年南京大学举办诗歌节,袁辉作为校友参赛,获得"诗韵风华奖"。"安然明物理,岁月且蹉跎""极望无云天静邃,不知何物动心扉"……他把自己喜欢的东西都写进去了,有春天与爱情,有崔健和康德,也有徐州的燕子楼。

曾经有亲戚热心帮忙介绍相亲对象,袁辉一概不理。他觉得,爱情要看缘分;他也没打算离开,"可能,现在的工作不是很适合谈婚论嫁"。

他有太多留下的理由:6年下来,他已经爱上了跟孩子们相处的时光;自己的教学探索也才刚刚起步;支教不是来体验生活,而是一份事业,开始了就不要轻易停下。

作家毛姆曾在小说《月亮与六便士》中,

将月亮比作对理想的追求，六便士比作现实多数人追求的金钱名利。袁辉的故事在网络传开后，一名网友留言：满地六便士，他抬头看见月亮。

Sixpence Is Everywhere, But He Looks Up and Sees the Moon

"Hand over your food!" cried a "robber" holding a "dagger" in his hand as he approached a primary school student. The student glanced at the packet of instant noodles in his hands, and, with almost no hesitation, threw it in the opposite direction and ran away.

The students watching bent over with laughter and clapped their hands for the calm and clever student on the stage.

This scene took place in the sixth grade classroom of Baishaping Primary School in Badong County of the Enshi Tujia and Miao Autonomous Prefecture in Hubei Province.

This is a class on safety. Outside the windows are rolling mountains. Inside the classroom, the green paint is peeling off the marked walls, and the cement floor is warping. For his class, Mr. Yuan Hui did not read from the text, but incorporated the main points into themed situational comedies. The students came on the stage to "play" the roles, and Yuan Hui would ask questions from time to time.

This type of instruction is often seen in Yuan Hui's class.

He graduated from the History Department of Nanjing University. He liked to study international politics at university. Upon graduation in 2012, he came to teach as a volunteer in a rural primary school more than 1,000 kilometers away from his hometown. He has been teaching

Sixpence Is Everywhere, But He Looks Up and Sees the Moon
满地六便士，他抬头看见月亮

for six years. Outside of class, children like to call him "Brother Yuan."

Brother Yuan has a peaceful and sunny face. At 30 years old, he has not purchased a house or a car, nor does he talk about love or getting married. Like many young people, Yuan Hui faced a choice when he graduated from university.

Before graduation, his supervisor wrote a letter recommending him for a job at a magazine in Nanjing. After the interview, the editor-in-chief was very satisfied. On the way back to his dormitory, Yuan Hui began thinking. He remembered his dream in high school. At that time, he had seen how students had crammed exhaustively for exams because of the teaching method, and Yuan Hui had wondered whether there were any other methods to enable students to not only master knowledge but also learn and grow happily. He'd dreamed that one day he could inject new energy into the development of education. In high school, the good teachers he met were both talented and approachable. Sometimes when he met them on campus, he would rush to hug them. That was when he thought that being a teacher was an excellent career choice.

He also remembered that compared with the bustling cities, he had always preferred the countryside. He'd lived in the countryside for some time when he was a child. He had fond memories of blue skies, white clouds and green trees, and also catching fish and crawfish. As he thought, the idea of going to the countryside to teach as a volunteer became clearer and more precise in his mind. In the end, he thanked his teacher and the magazine for the opportunity, packed his bags, and set off to the west.

At first, he went to look for teaching jobs at two schools: one in Mabian Yi Autonomous County in Sichuan Province, and one in Duyun County in Guizhou Province. Unfortunately, there were no teacher positions available there. He then remembered watching on TV the good deeds of Tan Dingcai, a "teacher on crutches" in Badong County, Hubei Province, who persisted in teaching at a rural school. So, after riding the train, the bus, and a three-wheeled cart, he finally arrived at Jiangjiawan School in the town of Qingtaiping where Tan Dingcai taught.

Looking at the young man in front of him, Tan Dingcai had his concerns. A famous university student from thousands of miles away came to teach at a school in a mountainous area? Did he understand this correctly? Tan asked him to think again and go back in order to find a good job. But Yuan had made up his mind. Qingtaiping had mountains with lush greenery, and the children's pure, clear eyes convinced him that this was where he wanted to stay. After the approval of the local education department, he found an empty classroom and settled down.

But being a volunteer teacher was not easy.

In class, the children were reserved; after class, some were mischievous. Yuan Hui looked into why they behaved this way. He found that this was a state-level impoverished county. Some students were left-behind children whose parents went to a different place to work, and some came from single-parent families.

"Under these circumstances, I must protect the children and allow them to feel nature, to help them relax and open their hearts while playing, and to improve their efficiency while studying so they can learn and be happy and vibrant." Yuan Hui thought about ways to improve their learning, and quickly designed a classroom teaching model that integrated the elements of situational comedies, or sitcoms.

In addition to teaching from the textbooks, Yuan Hui tried his best to give his students the same kind of comprehensive education as children receive in big cities. He once started a "classical culture class" to teach ancient poetry and Chinese. While teaching Jia Dao's poem "Swordsman," he gave sunglasses and toy swords as props to the students, and compared their performances, expressions and postures to see who best resembled an ancient swordsman.

He also led the students in writing modern poems and limericks, and also taught them painting. The children chose the best works of all the students and posted them on the classroom walls.

Gradually, teachers in nearby schools began to hear of Yuan at Jiangjiawan School and that his teaching method was very innovative. In 2014, Baishaping Primary School in the same town needed young teachers. The principal came to Yuan Hui and asked him to work in the school.

Baishaping Primary School has six grades with a total of 85 students. Yuan Hui joined the school, and is still there today. He serves as the sixth-grade teacher and also teaches fifth- and sixth-grade mathematics and moral education as well as third- and fourth-grade music classes. He has 31 classes a week, almost twice that of other teachers.

Recently, more than 4,700 sixth graders in Badong County took the mid-term exam. One-third of the students from Yuan Hui's class were among the top 1,000 in mathematics.

In addition to teaching six classes a day, Yuan Hui also teaches a "one-on-one class" after school.

Qingqing (pseudonym) turned 12 years old this year and is in the fifth grade at Baishaping Primary School. After only a few months of study at school, she developed a disability and had to be confined at home to a wheelchair. Yuan Hui could not bear to see her drop out of school, so he began going to her home two or three times every week to teach her, traveling 20 kilometers each time. The mountainous road is full of potholes, and he has broken two motorcycles going there, often riding in the wind and rain, but he has continued his one-on-one sessions with her to this day. His help has paid off. On every test, Qingqing's test scores are among the best in the class. Not only does he teach her free of charge, but he often brings dictionaries, books, milk and more to Qingqing. Qingqing's older sister has been admitted to a normal university, and, because of Yuan Hui's example, she plans to become a teacher after graduation. Qingqing's family is grateful to Yuan Hui, but Yuan Hui is humble. In his view, it is Qingqing who should be praised because although in a wheelchair, she is strong and eager to learn, and this exerts a positive influence on him.

Another student is Xiaoyong (pseudonym). Xiaoyong's mother left, and his father is paralyzed in bed. Seeing the challenges faced by Xiaoyong and his father, Yuan Hui bought instant noodles for them. After a while, Yuan Hui asked Xiaoyong if he had finished eating the noodles. Xiaoyong said that he had kept some and planned to eat them during the Spring Festival. Yuan Hui sighed with emotion seeing how difficult the boy's life was, but there was no trace of sadness on the child's face. Later, he bought some rice and noodles for Xiaoyong and his father. Also, seeing their sheets were dirty and worn out, he bought new ones for them. Yuan Hui's university classmates, other netizens and student volunteers from Huazhong Agricultural University pooled some money to help them. Now, Xiaoyong's family has a new TV set, and they are living a better life.

Yuan Hui posted the stories of Qingqing, Xiaoyong and other students on his WeChat Moments. Since 2016, student volunteers from Huazhong Agricultural University, South-Central Minzu University, Zhongnan University of Economics and Law, and Nanjing University have come to Baishaping Primary School to pair up with students to help them or to teach as volunteers during summer vacations.

Having been teaching for six years now, Yuan Hui still regards himself as a volunteer. This means that his income is not high. He only earns around 1,000 yuan per month, which is a quarter of what the other teachers receive. He values freedom and ease more than income. He can read his favorite books every day, breathe the fresh air, and climb the mountain every week. He thinks that this kind of rural life is simple, but rich. At the same time, he also has the friendship of the children. "I may bring them a different perspective, but they bring me joy and companionship. Without them, my life would be monotonous."

In the ten-square-meter-plus dormitory, there are five desks piled with books of philosophy, history, literature, etc. He also has gifts given to him by his students which are kept in a special storage box, most of which are greeting cards made by hand and bamboo pen holders. One student gave him a lollipop wrapped in paper, which Yuan Hui still has. Some of the greeting cards are pasted with flowers picked and dried by the children, and some are hand-painted with various small animals. The pen holders are engraved with flowers and grass, with words of blessings written on them.

The unique simplicity of these children in the mountainous area gives Yuan Hui a different memory.

While riding a bike one day, Yuan Hui fell to the ground and scraped his arm and face. The students found out about this and pooled their pocket money to buy some cotton swabs and iodine. They went to see him, and some took out a few cotton swabs and applied iodine, and asked if he was in pain. Others brought some special porridge for him that they'd been saving for a special occasion.

The life of a volunteer teacher is always challenging. Yuan Hui's father once came to visit him from Xuzhou, and saw that he had almost nothing but the bare walls in his room. He didn't even have tap water. In order to wash his clothes, Yuan Hui collected rainwater as it flowed from the eaves. The water had been stored for a long time and had black worms in it. He had to go to the top of the mountain to fetch spring water to drink and cook.

Seeing his son in this condition, he thought of the children of his colleagues, relatives and friends who, upon graduation from universities, stayed in big cities to get married and start their careers. He argued with Yuan Hui, but Yuan Hui still would not leave. He had

Sixpence Is Everywhere, But He Looks Up and Sees the Moon
满地六便士，他抬头看见月亮

made up his mind to teach here, saying that each person had his own lifestyle. He was needed here, he told his father. He was achieving a lot here, and he would continue to stay here.

The next day, his father, who had failed to persuade him to leave, went back home alone. He sent a text message on the way, saying, "Son, I'm sorry." Realizing that he was not around to take care of his parents, Yuan Hui replied, "I'm sorry, Dad." Soon after his father returned home, he sent Yuan Hui a thick overcoat. His parents never asked him to leave again.

Yuan Hui doesn't have a personal computer. He doesn't think that he needs it. There is a desktop computer in his office. He does online shopping only to buy books. His favorite book is Nietzsche's *Thus Spoke Zarathustra*. He has bought seven copies of different Chinese versions and reads them every day.

He maintains close ties with the outside world. His secondary school and university classmates have come to see him, and they often treat him to dinner. These classmates have also brought donations for children in need. Also paying close attention to Yuan Hui and sending charity school supplies to Yuan Hui's school have been the Hubei Provincial Committee of the Communist Youth League, the Enshi Prefectural Committee of the Communist Youth League, and the Badong County Party Committee.

He doesn't like to travel, but he climbs a mountain every week. On his WeChat Moments, there are children's smiling faces, the beautiful scenery of Badong, the towering green mountains and floating white clouds, and the ancient-style poems which he wrote.

In 2016, Nanjing University held a poetry festival. Yuan Hui participated as an alumnus and won the Poetry Charm Award. "Be clear about the innate laws of things, and time flies." "The boundless sky is cloudless and tranquil, but I don't know what stirs my heart." He writes about everything he likes, including spring and love, Cui Jian and Kant, and Xuzhou's Swallow Building.

Some of his relatives have tried to set up blind dates for him, but Yuan Hui ignores them, saying that love depends on fate. He does not plan to leave. "Maybe my current job is not suitable for marriage," he says.

He has many reasons to stay. For six years, he has loved spending time with the children. He has just started to explore his teaching model, and his volunteer work is not to experience life but to start a career — a career that he wants to pursue.

The British writer William Somerset Maugham once compared the moon to the pursuit of an ideal in his novel *The Moon and Sixpence*, where sixpence represented the money, fame, and wealth pursued by most people. After Yuan Hui's story was posted on the internet, a netizen left the message: Sixpence is everywhere, but he looks up and sees the moon.

Sixpence Is Everywhere, But He Looks Up and Sees the Moon
满地六便士,他抬头看见月亮

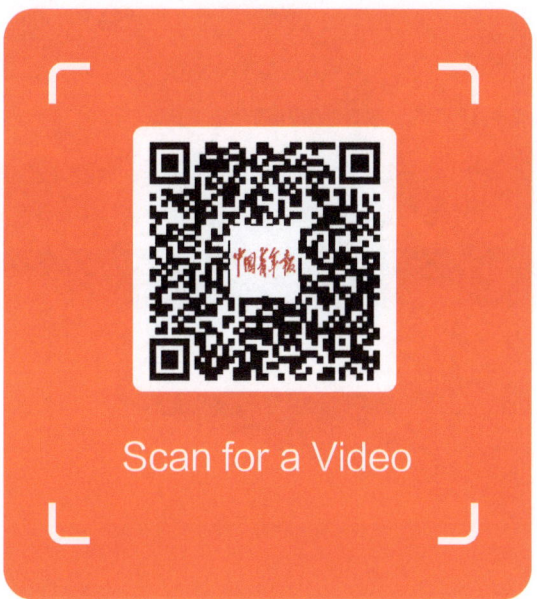

Scan for a Video

北漂国学老师之"道"

A Teacher of Traditional Chinese Culture in Beijing

作者：蒋　欣
翻译：吴爱俊

北漂国学老师之"道"

"请大家起立,肃整仪容,平心静气,向古圣先贤先师孔子行礼。"崔健笔直地站在课堂前,声音平缓地带着学员向投影上的孔子影像行鞠躬礼。这是他每次教国学课上下课前必行的礼节。"古圣先贤以礼乐教化世人,我们今天学习他们的经典,理所应当行之以礼节,以体现我们的恭敬和感恩。"

周三晚上 7 点,崔健的公益国学课准时在北京立水桥附近的一家中医理疗馆开讲。

他姐姐是这家理疗馆的主人。"课堂"的面积不大，三张理疗床，一张四方桌，一个木质书架几乎塞满整个房间，仅剩并不宽敞的过道供人通行。7个年轻人坐在过道的凳子上听课。20分钟前，理疗馆刚送走当日最后一位客人，整个房间里还飘着一股艾草的味道。

这已是崔健在过去两年中搬的第三个地方了。国学课从开办至今一直不收取任何费用，他也无力负担教室的租金，此前的状态基本是哪儿有免费场地就往哪儿搬。从北京的西边到北边，从四环挪到二环又到五环，大家能坚持听下来很不容易。

杜一帆从2016年9月开始跟着崔健上课，几乎每周都到场，他把这堂课称作"精神食粮"。下班后，他从北六环换乘两趟地铁赶来。他认为，这也是给国学老师最好的回报和尊重。上崔老师的课是重新认识自己的一个过程，而且他从未提过收钱的事。

当晚，崔健讲授的内容是《孟子》中的一篇，里面有一句话"行有不得，反求诸己"，被他奉为做人做事的准则。他说："凡是结果没有得到预期的效果，都应该反过来检视自己的不足。现在整个社会都活得太着急了，丢弃了很多中华文化中的智慧和原则，遗忘做人最根本的道义，而这些却不是钱可以买到的。"

崔健从事国学教育的时间并不长，此前只是自我研读。2015年2月，39岁的崔健辞去薪资优厚的工作，从南方来到北京：一者，因妻儿久居京城；二者，他也想"实现心中一直以来的理想"。那天，不常在微信分享个人生活状态的他，像个刚毕业冲劲十足北上奋斗的大学生，发了一条朋友圈："首都，我来了！"

来京之初，受朋友邀请，崔健每周四会同几位爱好国学的朋友交流，后不断有人慕名前来听课。

梁东兰和刚上高一的女儿关施君是崔健比较早的学员，即便是关施君中考前夕也都未落过一次课。他们喜欢崔老师的课，是因为崔老师讲课不是在简单解释句子的意思，复述前人的观点，他会结合古今背景，以社会现象、新闻热点为例帮助学生们理解，学

A Teacher of Traditional Chinese Culture in Beijing
北漂国学老师之"道"

以致用，在潜移默化间明白很多道理。

学习伊始，崔健就启发关施君："你要想一想，为什么学习国学？通过学习国学，你想得到什么？未来你想成为一个什么样的人？士不可以不弘毅。"

有一天上课前，15岁的关施君跑来告诉崔健，以后想报考北京大学中文系。崔健鼓励她："若你能心怀天下，愿尽一己之力对他人有帮助的时候，你的人生格局就会不一样。这条路不容易，任重而道远。"

梁东兰明显感觉到女儿的变化。"孩子以前一提到考试就闹心，现在她会把目标看得很长远，去思考人是为了什么而活，不单单是为了高考。"梁东兰说，《论语》早已成了女儿的枕边书，每天睡觉前都要翻上几页。

崔健很高兴，"国学曾经改变了我的人生状态，现在有更多人在其中受益。"

在很多学员眼中，崔健是个儒雅的老师，性格温和，为人谦逊。但十几年前，他也曾是个玩世不恭、浮躁世俗的顽固青年，大学毕业三年内换了近十份工作，喜欢抽烟、喝酒和泡吧，甚至一顿饭能喝三瓶红酒。

2003年年初，崔健前往新西兰留学，孤独与空虚之余，他开始接触国学。国外很难买到国学书籍，他就在网上查找、阅读，有时盯着屏幕上那一句句简短的话陷入长久思考。2005年冬天，他首次回国探亲，看到城市空气中弥漫着灰尘，街上车辆经常堵作一团，喇叭声响个不停，朋友聚会聊的话题无非是房子、票子、车子……

崔健想逃，哪怕亲人都在上海，他也想赶紧逃回南半球那个不属于自己的地方。他说，在国外没有什么娱乐，不少人对中国的传统文化和礼仪典故都十分感兴趣，有些人因为这些共同的爱好，不时聚在一起探讨、交流。他认为，西方理论教的多是方法，为"术"；而中华文化的经典讲的则是根源，是"本"。可是我们现在的社会与人心正走在离"本"越来越远的路上。

2012年，崔健做出了回国的决定。他认为，老祖宗的智慧根源于这片土地，寻找与探索经典，继承与发扬文化，都应该发生在这里。在北京的头一年，因为一直致力于公益课程，他基本属于零收入状态。租房和生活费用，只靠太太的收入及父母不时的接济，一家人过得很清贫。他也会偶感在孤军奋战，甚至曾遇到警察找上门来，查他是不是在搞什么不法活动。"如果是为了钱，或者介意贫穷与质疑，我就不会选择做现在这件事。我的课欢迎任何人来听，哪怕你只是路过。"

北京海淀区星火小学向崔健递出了橄榄枝，以200元一节课的费用聘请他为学校"课后一小时"的国学课老师。崔健当时考虑了很久，倒不是因为钱，而是怕教不好孩子们。学校的初衷就是想先教会孩子做人，这与崔健的初心不谋而合。每节课的最后10分钟，崔健会教孩子们一些基本的国民礼仪：吃饭的时候要端碗，不要发出声音；给人端水端饭的时候要用双手；咳嗽或打喷嚏的时候要捂住嘴巴……

第一个学期结束后，崔健给学校交了一份课业总结：经常有家长抱怨自己的孩子有这样或那样的问题，可又有几个家长反思过形成这些问题的根源在哪里呢？孩子只是我们的复印件。现在，这些复印件上有了瑕疵，我们该从原件上着手还是去复印件上折腾呢？校领导看后十分重视，将这份总结转发到全校教师群里供大家学习。

之后崔健又在学校开设"齐家读书会"课堂，在全校范围内招募20个家庭，每周一课后由家长带着孩子一同参与。有家长听完第一节课后告诉崔健："您这堂课讲得我的心特别疼，我才发现原来那些问题都是我的问题，我回去后一定好好反省自己。"

刚回国的时候，一位长者告诉崔健："这个世间需要的不是抱怨，而是坚持做自己该做的，最终找到两个认同的人站在你的两边；慢慢地，他们也能找到同样的人站在自己的两边，那时就能形成善的力量，改变一方的风气，为社会注入一股清流，这远比抱怨有用得多。"

崔健觉得，自己的国学造诣还不够深。"如果用一杯水来形容，我现在也刚刚没过杯底而已，离满溢还有很远。只有不断地学习和实践，才能达到知行合一的境界，否则，人的内心就会如干涸的大地，因缺乏滋润而龟裂。"他从不把学员当学生，在他看来，这些听他讲课的人更像朋友，大家一起相互督促与进步。

他很享受这个过程，教学相长就像在凿墙一般，有时很用劲也只能敲掉几块墙皮，但只要坚持，总有凿通的时候。"那一瞬间，你似乎能听到墙被打通后'嘭'的一声，原来的障碍没有了，通了以后才会看到里面最美丽的画，那样的时刻是最令人欣喜的。"

2016年12月12日，崔健完成了这学期最后一堂"齐家读书会"的教学。课程结束时，他再次分享了"士不可以不弘毅，任重而道远"。这是《论语》中他最喜欢的一句话。

那天晚上，崔健收到了"齐家读书会"微信群里众多家长的致谢，其中有一位家长写道："我问孩子最大的收获是什么，他说懂得了很多做人的道理。"

A Teacher of Traditional Chinese Culture in Beijing

"Please stand up, have a neat appearance, be calm and salute Confucius," says Cui Jian standing in front of his students as straight as an iron rod. He leads them in bowing to the image of Confucius on the overhead projector. This is the routine before he begins his traditional Chinese culture lessons. "Just as our ancestors educated people by advocating rituals, we shall also follow rituals to show respect and gratitude."

Cui's traditional Chinese culture class is held at 7 p.m. on Wednesdays in a TCM physiotherapy center in the Lishuiqiao neighborhood of Beijing.

His sister is the owner of the physiotherapy center. It is not big and therefore appears almost full with three physiotherapy beds, a table and a wooden bookshelf. There is only a narrow aisle for people to pass through, in which seven young people sit and listen. Twenty minutes ago, the last client left with the smell of moxa still lingering in the air.

This is the third place Cui has moved to in the past two years. Since the beginning, his traditional Chinese courses have been free to attend, and thus he cannot afford to rent a classroom. He had been moving all around town to wherever he could find a rent-free location, from the west part of Beijing to the north, from the fourth ring road to the second ring road and then to the fifth ring road. It is not easy for students to continue coming to his lessons.

Du Yifan has been attending Cui's class since September 2016 and attends almost every week, which he calls "spiritual nourishment." He takes the subway from the north sixth ring road after work. He thinks that persistence is the best way to repay and respect his teacher. Cui's class is helpful for people looking to rediscover themselves, and he has never mentioned any tuition fee.

One evening, Cui Jian gave a lecture on a passage from *Mencius*, in which he hailed one sentence as a code of conduct: One should reflect on oneself whenever one fails to get an expected result. He said, "If our expectation cannot be met, we need to examine our shortcomings. All of society is so anxious to succeed, but ignores traditional Chinese values and wisdom, which are assets that cannot be purchased."

Cui learned traditional Chinese culture on his own. He started teaching Chinese culture several years ago. In February 2015, he quit his high-salary job at the age of 39 and came to Beijing from the south. He wanted to live together with his wife and son, who had been staying in Beijing. He also wanted to fulfill a lifelong dream of living and working in Beijing. Although he seldom posted anything on WeChat Moments in the past, he decided to share something the day he arrived: "Here I come, Beijing!" He was like an ambitious college graduate ready to fight for his career in Beijing.

When he first arrived, he was invited by some friends to talk about traditional Chinese culture together on Thursdays. After that, more and more people came to listen to their talks.

Liang Donglan and her daughter Guan Shijun were among Cui's first students. Even during the days as Guan's high school entrance examination approached, she did not miss any courses. They like Cui's course because he combines ancient topics with current affairs to help students understand the classics, enabling them to apply what they've learned into practice. He does not simply explain the classics or retell the opinions of ancient sages.

In those early days, Cui had told Guan, "You should ask yourself several questions: Why do you think you need to learn traditional Chinese culture? What do you want to acquire through this course? What kind of person do you want to be? A true scholar must have perseverance and ambition."

One day before class, 15-year-old Guan told Cui that she wanted to apply to the Chinese Department of Peking University. Cui encouraged her, "If you have a broad mind and are willing to help others, your life will be unlike any other. It will be a long road to traverse before you achieve this goal."

Liang Donglan could see the changes taking place in her daughter. "Previously, my child was always worried about exams, but now she has a broader perspective, focusing on the meaning of life rather than on simply exams." Her daughter always keeps *The Analects* by her bedside so that she can read a few pages before sleeping.

Cui says that traditional Chinese culture has changed his life, and he can see more people benefiting from it.

His students describe Cui as erudite, gentle, and humble. However,

A Teacher of Traditional Chinese Culture in Beijing
北漂国学老师之"道"

over a decade ago, he was stubborn, cynical, impetuous and flippant. Within only three years after graduation he'd changed jobs nearly ten times. He liked smoking, drinking, and visiting nightclubs. He could even drink three bottles of wine during one meal.

In early 2003, he went to New Zealand to study. Alone and empty, he began learning traditional Chinese culture. He found it difficult to buy these types of books overseas, so he would often get on the internet and search and read whatever he could find. Sometimes he would simply see phrases on the screen and become lost in deep thought. In the winter of 2005 he returned to China to visit relatives, and saw the vehicles in the city covered with dust, traffic jams, and heard the constant blaring of horns. When going out with friends, all they could talk about were houses, money, cars ....

Although all of his relatives were in Shanghai, Cui looked forward to returning to New Zealand. He said that there was a lack of exposure to Chinese culture overseas, but many people were very interested in traditional Chinese culture and rituals. Many would get together to discuss this. He has come to the conclusion that Western culture focuses mainly on method and "techniques," while Chinese culture focuses more on the roots of something and the "essence." However, Cui believes nowadays people are gradually stepping father and farther away from these "roots."

In 2012, Cui Jian decided to return to China. He believed that since the wisdom of Chinese forefathers originated from the land, this was the place where he should explore and carry forward Chinese culture. During his first year in Beijing, he started a free course. He had no income, so he had to rely on his wife's earnings and his parents' financial aid to afford the rent and living expenses. His family lived a poor life. He sometimes felt alone in this endeavor, and the police have even come to him several times to investigate if he was involved in any illegal activities. "If I cared about money, poverty, and the suspicions of others, I would not do what I'm doing now. Anyone is welcome to listen to my class, even if you are just passing by."

The Xinghuo Primary School in Haidian District invited Cui to teach traditional Chinese culture and paid him 200 yuan per class. Cui was very hesitant because he was worried if he could teach the students well. He finally agreed when he found that the school's plan for the course was to teach children how to be good members of society, which was exactly Cui's aspiration. In the last ten minutes of each lesson, Cui would teach the children basic traditional manners, such as holding a bowl while eating, avoiding making sounds while eating, giving others bowls and cups with both hands, and covering your mouth when coughing or sneezing.

At the end of the first semester, Cui submitted a summary of his impressions, which said, "Parents often complain about their children's problems, but how many of them have tried to discover what has caused these problems? Our children imitate us. When problems occur in our children, shall we look for the cause from our children or from ourselves?" Having read Cui's comments, the school leader thought Cui had made an important point and posted the summary in a WeChat group for all the teachers to read.

Afterward, Cui Jian started a "Family Reading Class" in school, where

A Teacher of Traditional Chinese Culture in Beijing
北漂国学老师之"道"

he invited 20 families to join his lesson after class every Monday. Some parents told Cui after the first lesson, "Your lesson made me sad because now I know that I am to be blamed for my child's problems. After I go home, I try to reflect on my own behavior."

When Cui had just returned to China, one senior told him, "What this world needs is less complaining, and more insisting on doing something. In doing so, you'll find two people who share your same principles standing by your side, and this can affect positive change. In time, those two people will gather people of similar views standing by their sides. In time, you can inject real change into society. This is far more useful than complaining."

Cui Jian felt his knowledge of traditional Chinese culture was far from adequate. "If my knowledge in this field is compared to a cup of water, I feel it just covers the bottom and is far from overflowing. Only by continuous study and practice can we achieve the unity between knowledge and action. Otherwise, our minds will become as infertile as arid land due to lack of nourishment." He has never considered those who study under him as "students," but more like friends, as they all supervise and progress and learn from each other.

He enjoys this process very much, saying that teaching and learning is a two-way process, "like carving a hole in a wall. Sometimes, even with great force, you can only scratch off a patch of paint. But as long as you persist, the wall eventually will be broken through. At that moment, you'll hear a 'bang!' after the wall is broken. The obstacles are gone. After it is broken, you'll see the most beautiful paintings inside. That is the moment that is most gratifying."

On December 12, 2016, Cui Jian finished his last lesson of the semester. At the end of the class, he shared his favorite quote from *The Analects*: "A scholar must have ambition and perseverance because they have a long way to go and will shoulder great responsibility."

That night, Cui received many thanks from his students' parents via WeChat. One of the parents wrote, "When I asked my child: 'What was the greatest thing you learned?' He told me that he now understands the principles of what it means to be a human being."

小保安闯出大名堂

An Ambitious Security Guard

作者：田文生
翻译：吴爱俊

小保安闯出大名堂

穿着便衣,朱良玉和往常一样,在北京某商场广场南门附近执勤。一个40岁左右的中年妇女引起了他的注意。这名妇女虽然在逛街,但手里总拿着个大围脖,压根儿不看货物一眼,眼神只瞄着人。

从一楼到二楼,再到三楼、四楼,最终又折回一楼,这名妇女反复走了好几趟,最后到三楼的羊毛衫柜台停住。面对着年轻女顾客,她用围脖挡住手,没几秒钟,她肩膀猛然向上一抖。

"小偷得手了!"朱良玉判断。他上前一把抓住妇女的肩膀,对方却转过身朝朱良玉脸上吐了口唾沫,"你神经病,我才不是小偷,我是你们的上帝!"朱良玉连拖带拽,好不容易将她带到保卫部,却没发现失主的钱包,朱良玉只好向她赔礼道歉。

感觉憋屈的朱良玉没死心,他跑到监控室来来回回地查看录像。原来,女贼也讲究配合，拿到钱包后，她第一时间将它甩在地上，被接应的同伙顺势捡走。朱良玉的轴劲儿上来了，他留心了半个月，终于等到这名妇女重施故伎，赶忙带人抓了个正着，把她和三个同伙一起送上警车。

但凡遇上朱良玉巡逻，辖区里的不法分子掉头就跑。因为长得黑，他们还给他起了个外号——"黑猫警长"。干保安的25年里，朱良玉带队抓获各类犯罪嫌疑人624人，破获盗窃案160多起，扑灭火灾10余起，挽回经济损失500多万元。

"战争年代靠解放军，和平年代靠警察，日常生活就得靠保安。"在朱良玉看来，涉及安保的很多问题，如果在发生前期不及时处理就会造成大麻烦。他对自己有个要求——做辖区第一个发现问题的人。

来北京之前，他对保安的职业没什么概念。高考落榜后，他铆足劲儿创业，在山东老家干养殖，本以为能搭上时代的顺风车成为万元户，结果遇上一场大暴雨，淋跑了鱼，淋死了鸡，也浇灭了他的创业梦。要账的人隔三差五找上门来，朱良玉卖了家里唯一值钱的牛，攥着300元开始北漂。

他原本以为，这工作戴大檐帽、穿笔挺的制服，应该和警察差不多，挺有威严。没想到上班第一天，他照着流程给小区居民敬礼，请他们出示证件，一名女同志直接嚷嚷"甭理他，我们进去，这就是看门狗"。

朱良玉蒙了，差点儿冲上去和他们好好争论一番，但想起公司"打不还手、骂不还口"的工作方针，只好忍下来。事后，他拿到了自己职业生涯的第一个奖状，是保安公司颁发的"委屈奖"——风格高尚奖。那段时间，他感觉这份工作实在不好干。

转折点出现在一天夜里12点多，他一个人从执勤单位蹓回宿舍时。那天天气格外冷，路上也几乎看不见人。进了巷子，他总觉得背后有人跟着，后来发现是位30多岁的大姐。对方态度诚恳地说，自己是附近的工人，下夜班回家，走这段路总觉得心里慌，看朱良玉穿一身保安制服，跟着他才觉得踏实。

"我也不是一个只会遭人白眼的保安

嘛。"朱良玉想，这份工作并不是时刻处在阴暗的角落里无人问津，小保安也能带给很多人极大的安全感，换一种"高大上"的理解，保安也是社会建设中不可或缺的一分子。

朱良玉曾在北京海淀区翠微大厦带队执勤。因为地形复杂，这里还一度被定义为"最令人头疼"的安保区域。那时候，商场刚开业，一帮专吃"开业饭"的盗贼经常光顾，一天遇到四五起盗窃案都是常事儿。为此，朱良玉时刻紧绷着神经，从发现问题到等待下手，常常一盯就是两三个小时。

一次，翠微大厦某间财务室被盗走20万元现金，海淀公安分局成立专案组前来逐个排查。大厦人流密集，人员流动频繁，他们只能看监控录像。监控放到凌晨的一个画面，一名男子抱着纸箱走出财务室，协助办案的朱良玉一下喊出了该男子的名字。原来，这是个最近常来翠微大厦蹓跶的无业青年，每天雷打不动巡逻的朱良玉对此人再熟悉不过。

有了朱良玉带队，翠微大厦附近的治安状况让人踏实。有记者来试探，暗地里以消费者身份故意在商场里丢了三次包，可每次还没走，就被保安队员追上来提醒。一篇名为《在翠微大厦想丢东西都难》的报道由此而生。

抓贼看起来风光，但实际上危险重重。朱良玉的腿上有道长长的伤疤，是跟小偷搏斗时被刀刺伤的。他断了不法分子的财路，就有人"不让他好过"。朱良玉被人在路上堵过，家门被铁丝和木棍团团塞住，窗户还被人用砖头砸出个大窟窿。

在平日，保安需要耐得住寂寞，按部就班站好岗，大部分时间比较枯燥；但一遇见突发险情就是十万火急。"天不怕，地不怕，就怕晚上来电话"。辖区突然起火的情况他没少遇见过。一次，附近的地下室失火，下了班的朱良玉立刻赶回现场。看见浓烟弥漫的地下室，他二话没说，拎着两个灭火器钻进了浓烟。那次，他用掉七个灭火器，身上被灼伤好几处。

普遍来说，保安工作门槛不高，学到

的技能也相对有限。"打铁还需自身硬",他硬着头皮迈进学校学习。值班的空当,他拿出书来读。他还买了随身听,在路上边听边学。从经济学到行政法,朱良玉一一攻克,他先后考取专科、本科、研究生学历。

他总认为,年轻人跟着自己当几年保安,如果没出息,那自己就是在误人子弟。所以,他总鼓励手下的人学习。他管理的辖区的保安队员里,60多人考了大专以上的文凭,20多人被评为区级以上先进工作者,有40多人先后被提升到保安管理岗位,还有人转行当起老板。

励志故事的背后也有现实社会沉重的一面。朱良玉现在还住在租来的房子里,直到七个月前,他才搬离地下室。儿子刚上大学,妻子没有工作,很多年来,他们全部的收入就是朱良玉每月五六千元的工资。他承认,就目前来说,这项职业的社会认可度远远不够。有时候他也很心痛,队里的小伙子交了女朋友,不敢说自己的具体工作,因为说了很可能就会被分手。

他开始琢磨怎么能切实提升保安的职业荣誉感。中国的保安有450多万人，是不可或缺的治安力量。但从实际来讲，大部分迈入这个岗位的年轻人一开始都是因为无路可走。

"保安上升通道窄，付出多，得到的相对少。"朱良玉曾把建议带上两会，呼吁提高保安的工资待遇，加强保安权益保障，稳定保安队伍。他想让老百姓看到，想让更多的企业知道，其实保安不仅是站岗、巡逻、押运、放哨的小角色，这些人长期驻守一线，对地域熟悉，侦查经验也丰富，他们能够参与更多的安全防范工作，比如对大楼重要部位的评测和安装防盗系统的评估。

An Ambitious Security Guard

Zhu Liangyu is a security guard, and one day he was patrolling in plain clothes near the south end of a commercial plaza in Beijing. Suddenly, a 40-year-old woman caught his attention. She was standing with an oversized scarf in her hand, and was not looking at the commodities for sale, but was instead looking only at the people.

He followed her as she went from the first floor to the fourth floor, and then back to the first floor. She continued this routine several times. Finally, she stopped at the sweater counter on the third floor. She faced a young girl with her hands hidden by the scarf. Several seconds later, she jerked her shoulder up.

"The thief succeeds," Zhu thought. He rushed to her and grabbed her by the shoulder, but the woman turned around and spat out towards him. "You maniac! I'm not a thief!" Zhu took her to the security department, but after searching her he didn't find anything stolen. Zhu was forced to apologize.

Zhu felt aggrieved, but didn't give up. He ran to the monitor room where he replayed the video many times. It turns out that after stealing the young girl's wallet, the woman threw it on the ground where her accomplice later took it away. Zhu then watched this area for half a month, and finally spotted the woman trying to do the same trick again. With the help of his colleagues, Zhu caught her and her three accomplices on the spot, and took them to the police.

Any wrongdoer in the community is afraid of meeting Zhu Liangyu. Because of his dark complexion, he has earned the nickname "black cat police chief." He has been a security guard for 25 years and has arrested 624 criminal suspects, investigated over 160 theft and robbery cases, put out over ten fires, and recovered economic losses worth over five million yuan.

"During wartime, we need soldiers. During times of peace, we need police officers. Day to day, we need security guards." Zhu believes that if any small security problems are not attended to in a timely way, they may escalate. He constantly pushes himself to be the first to discover any existing issues in his patrol area.

Before coming to Beijing, he didn't know what a security guard did. Although he failed the College Entrance Examination, he was still motivated to start a business in his hometown in Shandong Province. He was working in the breeding industry and dreamed of becoming wealthy. However, a heavy rainstorm made his fish escape and drowned his chickens, thereby ruining his start-up business dream. From time to time, his creditors would come to his house to demand their money back. Zhu Liangyu had to sell the only valuable asset he had left — his cow — and shortly afterwards left for Beijing with only 300 yuan in his pocket.

As a security guard, he thought he would be as awe-inspiring as a policeman in his neat uniform and wide-brimmed hat. But on the first day, after saluting the community residents and asking to see their certificates, one woman shouted, "Ignore the guard dog. Let's go in."

An Ambitious Security Guard
小保安闯出大名堂

Zhu was shocked and was ready to argue with them, but he remembered his company slogan: "Never argue or fight back." He had to bear the unfair treatment. Afterwards, he was awarded the first honorary credential in his career—Nobility Prize for Bearing Unfairness. During that period, he felt this job was not as easy as he had previously thought.

A turning point came one night. It was freezing cold. He was returning to his dormitory alone after work and there was no one in the street. After entering a small alley, he felt someone was following him. He turned and spoke with her, and found that she was a woman in her thirties, and a worker nearby. She'd been walking home after her night shift, and was feeling uneasy as she always does when walking alone. But she said when she saw Zhu in his security guard uniform, she followed him, and felt more secure.

That was when Zhu realized the importance of security guards, and that they were not just unnoticed workers in a corner. They can bring a sense of safety to others, and were an essential part of society.

He once led his team to patrol around the Cuiwei Building in Haidian District, Beijing. Because of the complex layout, it was considered one of the toughest security jobs. After the mall was open, four or five cases of theft occurred almost every day. Because of this, Zhu was on high alert every day, and it often took him two to three hours of constant surveillance before he could finally catch thieves in the act.

One day, 200 thousand yuan was stolen from the accounting department of the Cuiwei Building. The Haidian Police Station established a task force to investigate the case. Since the area around the building was crowded every day, they watched the monitor video to discover clues. As the video played one scene at midnight, they saw a man carrying a box out of the accounting department. Zhu immediately shouted out the man's name. Zhu was familiar with the young man, who had no job and had been hanging around there recently.

Thanks to Zhu and his team, the area around the Cuiwei Building became a safe place. Once, a journalist came disguised as a customer and dropped his wallet on purpose three times. Each time, a security guard alerted him he'd dropped his wallet. Because of this, a story was published, entitled "Hard to Lose Things in Cuiwei."

Arresting thieves looks cool, but is dangerous. There is still a long scar on his leg from a knife wound when he fought with a thief. Because he often apprehended or stopped criminals, they often sought him to take their revenge. Zhu has been ambushed on the road, and the door of his house has been blocked with iron wire and wooden poles, and his windows have been broken with bricks.

Security guards often find their job tedious because they follow the same routine almost every day. But once an emergency occurs, the situation will become tense. "The only thing that frightens us is telephone calls at night." Zhu has encountered quite a few fires in the neighborhood. When there was a fire in a basement nearby, Zhu hurried to the scene, even though he was off duty. Seeing the heavy smoke, he did not hesitate to rush into it with two extinguishers to put out the fire. He used up seven extinguishers and suffered several burns

An Ambitious Security Guard
小保安闯出大名堂

on his body.

Generally speaking, being a security guard does not require high qualifications, and the skills they can learn from the job are limited. Zhu knew that if he wanted to improve himself, he'd have to study on his own. He began taking classes. During his free time, he would read books. He also bought a Walkman and would listen to lessons on the way to and from work. He studied courses from economics to administrative laws, and gained a degree from a junior college and then a bachelor's and a master's.

He also encourages his young subordinates to keep learning. Of those on his team, over 60 have graduated from junior college or above, over 20 have been awarded the title of "Outstanding Workers Above the District Level," and over 40 have been promoted to management personnel. Some others have started their own businesses.

Zhu still faces some difficulties in life. He lives in a rented apartment. He moved here from a basement seven months ago. He is the sole breadwinner of the family as his son has just begun to study in university and his wife has no job. Zhu's monthly salary of five to six thousand yuan has to cover the family's every expense. He admits that a security guard in China is not an attractive job. He felt sad when he learned that some young men on his team did not dare tell their girlfriends about their job for fear they might break up with them. Then he began to consider how to improve people's understanding of this profession. There are over 4.5 million security guards in China who are an inalienable part of China's security force. But the truth is that most young people do this job because they have no other choice.

"Security guards have to do a lot with a low salary and have fewer opportunities to be promoted." Zhu submitted proposals to increase the payment of security guards and ensure their rights and interests to the National People's Congress & the Chinese People's Political Consultative Conference. He hopes to let more people and enterprises realize that the duties of a security guard are not confined to guarding, patrolling and escorting. Because they are stationed for long periods of time, they are very familiar with the neighborhood. They also have a lot of experience dealing with criminal activities. For these reasons, they can be given greater roles to play in security work, such as assessing the security conditions of vital areas of a building or installing anti-theft systems.

An Ambitious Security Guard
小保安闯出大名堂

Scan for a Video

火雷兄弟，江湖再见

See You Again, Fire and Thunder Brothers

作者：尹海月
翻译：韩芙芸

火雷兄弟，江湖再见

从武汉雷神山医院撤离之前，一小队工人举办了一个小型的生日会。这是一个叫徐德军的年轻人的32岁生日。工友们萍水相逢，还是劳务公司老板通过工人们上交的身份证得知了他的生日。

2020年3月30日这天，有近20名工友为他庆生。一位叫周凯的工人自掏腰包订了一个蛋糕。新冠肺炎疫情期间，蛋糕店大都不营业，他终于从网上查到一家，花了380元，蛋糕尺寸是14英寸。订完他又觉得有点儿小，后悔没买个三层的。听说徐德军喜欢打牌，他选了一个"麻将蛋糕"，上面摆着用巧克力制作的"东""西""南""北""中""发"麻将牌，还有黄澄澄的金元宝。

在医院附近一个闲置的厂区里，摆好这个充满发财渴望的生日蛋糕，这些工人就着花生米喝着啤酒，又跳又笑，唱起了生日歌。

See You Again, Fire and Thunder Brothers
火雷兄弟，江湖再见

有人还在脸上贴了五星红旗图案，这图标是欢送医务人员留下来的——3月29日起，在雷神山医院服务的外省医疗队陆续撤离，这是疫情得到缓解的好消息。

徐德军在一家建筑公司做管理，常年在工地跟工人打交道，这次是来当工人。生日会上，他按照工友们设计的动作，仰着脸，叼着烟，大摇大摆入场，和大家一起高唱《我的好兄弟》。他说，这是自己"一生中最难忘的生日"。

工友许新焰把过程拍了下来，剪辑成小视频，末尾写着"江湖再见"。他很喜欢这句话，觉得有"侠义气"。

另一位工人钟巍巍则说，大家都是"经历过生死"的战友了。

武汉1月23日因疫情"封城"，随后决定建设收治新冠肺炎患者的板房医院——火神山医院和雷神山医院，仅十天完工。到4月15日，收治过5071名患者的两所医院关闭。承建方中建三局总经理陈卫国介绍，总计有3.5万名工人参建，其中近2万名从外地赶来。工人们归属不同的劳务公司管理，从四面八方集合到这个曾令无数人牵肠挂肚的工地上。

在工地短暂休息时，五湖四海的工人们才有机会了解彼此，拉几句家常，手里的烟你递给我，我递给你，话题主要就那几个：家在哪里，家里几口人，这次干完后又要去哪里。

下一个工地在哪里是谈论最多的话题。如果疫情没有发生，他们本来会在不同地方建设高楼、地铁或者桥梁。很多人的车里总是装着切割机、电钻、钳子、螺丝刀之类的工具，哪里有活儿就把铺盖卷搬到哪里。

在火神山医院和雷神山医院工地上能找到不同职业的从业者：公务员、货车司机、小学教师，还有生意人和外卖小哥。

武汉人钟巍巍是家族总动员，同去的还有他的父亲、哥哥、舅舅和表弟。钟巍巍喜欢工地，工地上抬头一看就是天，想唱歌的时候就吼几句，都是干活儿的人，也不用搞得"那么体面"。

32岁的他从15岁起就跑工地，和武汉一起成长，帮它建起一所所学校，一条条地

See You Again, Fire and Thunder Brothers
火雷兄弟，江湖再见

铁轨道。计划今年年底通车的武汉第 11 座大桥——青山长江大桥也有他的参与。他曾在那里高空作业，几十米高的吊篮下，长江昼夜奔流。

当劳务公司老板找人去援建火神山医院时，钟巍巍和哥哥钟欣欣立即答应了。他们第二天就去了火神山医院工地，干了两天，又赶往 32 公里外的雷神山医院。

到达雷神山第五天，钟巍巍突然有了"一点儿小感触"，当时，他站在医院屋顶上施工，一眼望过去，看到下面全是脑袋，他的眼泪一下子出来了，"当时想，还是中国人团结，我平时很少对这些东西'那个'，但那是一触即发的。"承载万人的工地上都是一样的反光服和黄色安全帽。起初，领班们无法辨认本班组的四五十名工友，就让大家在安全帽上写上班组名称，时间长了，各位工长看到眼睛就能认出是自家工友。

43 岁的雷海涛是武汉江夏区第五中学的一名体育教师。他的工作是为 30 多名工友负责后勤保障。每天早上，他用体育课的"稍息、立正"号令催促大家集合开工。工人们尊他一声"雷老师"。

在雷神山工地时，雷海涛想尽办法劝说一位货车司机留在工地帮工，让疲惫的工友们得以在车里休息。工地上人多，工具常常换着用，转眼就会不见，货车成了放置电缆、电线、施工工具的小仓库。工地上没有开水，车里备了水壶，还有从周边小商店抢购的泡面、提神的零食。

为了给工友们多留出半小时休息时间，雷海涛每天中午提前去食堂排队，将盒饭提到工地。他说，疫情发生后，自己一直想做些事。除了记录考勤，雷海涛还负责为队友去仓库取施工工具，去一次仓库来回要走20多分钟。哪怕只是一个裁纸刀、几个螺丝钉，他也会跑一趟。对不认识的工具，这位体育老师就在网上搜索对应的图片，记住型号，再去仓库里找。闲下来时，雷海涛就给同组的工友打下手。有工友累得靠墙站着睡觉，还有的吃完饭饭盒都没收拾就歪着睡着了。看到这样的场景，他总是不忍心。

出于抗疫需要，雷神山医院的规模三次扩大，一度边建设边收治患者，交付后仍需工人负责后期维保工作。钟巍巍参建的病房区域基本完工后，需要技术熟练、能熬夜、年龄不超过40岁的工人参与后期维保，兄弟俩叫来镇上相熟的工友。钟巍巍把公司跟他们讲过的承诺复述了一遍：如果感染病毒，国家给治；万一不在了，国家给补偿。两天时间有近百人报名。

"感染了就治，人的一生就这样，我感觉没什么好遗憾的。"许新焰被钟巍巍喊去时，他觉得这是看得起自己，"需要我过来，我肯定来。"

有一次，室外排污系统出现故障，需要有人钻到地下将破损管子掏出，但里面散落着病人的粪便。钟巍巍记得，他手下的两位师傅什么话都没说，穿上防护服就爬了进去。在地下移动时尤其要小心翼翼，以免弄破防护服。其中一位工友师傅则回忆，当时班组接到任务，三天之内必须把负责区域内的排水处理好，任务来了就要干，"根本就没有想那么多"。

有时，看他们蹲着做事很累，会有护士拿来凳子，送来水果、牛奶和蛋糕。在病房里一个人维修不便，有病人会从床上爬下来递工具。还有人向他们鞠躬，给他们竖起大拇指。

许新焰将自己的作品留在了雷神山医院。他从小喜欢画画儿，干活儿无聊时，就画画儿打发时间，身边朋友、家乡风景、名人肖像，他什么都画，没有老师教，他就在网上看教程跟着学。看到有医务人员在医院走廊的白墙上画漫画，他也开始动笔。他把新冠病毒画成手持镰刀的怪物，迎战的是工地上常见的搅拌车和挖掘机。还有外地医护人员请他画出家乡的地标建筑，中建三局的工作人员也请他给工人们画漫画形象，比如，一群工人手持盾牌，类似"复仇者联盟"，取名"抗疫联盟"。他在这段时间完成的画作不到20幅，同其他作品一起分布在两三百米的病房走廊里，有工友觉得看着心里轻松，"人走到里头，没有恐惧"。这些画让徐德军觉得大家"真真正正地在医院建设中或者抗疫过程中存在过"。

因为学生要开"空中课堂"，雷海涛老师2月8日结束了他的工地生涯。但他们的

See You Again, Fire and Thunder Brothers
火雷兄弟，江湖再见

联系并未中断，有工友结束工期后驱车去找他聊天。

一位工人记得，曾有孩子打电话问工地上的爸爸"你是英雄吗"？爸爸反问"啥才是英雄"，儿子回答"医护人员"。

回家乡后，赵全喜也被几位朋友称赞是武汉回来的英雄。武汉工友听说他们远道而来，特地跟他们道谢，和他们合影，这让赵全喜感动。

"说不定若干年以后，还有个别的啥事情，我们也遇到这种，人家会来帮我们。但是像这种瘟疫，这么一次就够了，希望再不要发生。"他说。

因为参建医院，钟巍巍第一次在电视台的新闻里露了脸。他承认自己高兴得两晚没睡着觉，5分15秒的视频，他循环播放了不下50次。他的理解是，"一般只有名人、企业家才有资格（上电视），像我们这种普通建筑工人哪有什么资格？"

田魁也成了女儿的榜样。在微信朋友圈发布显示雷神山医院的定位后，他获得女儿同学家长一个点赞的"大拇指"，还有两个字：

英雄。上小学的女儿还对同学骄傲地说，爸爸在武汉。

"我们曾经奋斗过，为武汉人民作过贡献，也尽了自己的力量。用他们的话说，可以跟自己子孙吹牛的。其实大家也不是说要什么荣誉，我们真希望有一个纪念、有个念想的东西。"雷海涛曾就这个问题跟劳务公司老板交流过两三次，两人达成了共识：以公司的名义为每人制作一枚纪念章。

4月21日，一位工人收到一张明信片，拍照发到了微信群里。长方形的明信片背面是一张标着"致敬最美建设者"的工人肖像，正面写了几行赞美的话，结尾写着："感谢！火雷兄弟！致敬！平凡英雄！"落款为"中建三局火神山医院、雷神山医院建设指挥部"。

火神山和雷神山施工进度最受瞩目的时候，参建者的身影曾出现在几千万人在线观看的"云直播"里。不过，摄像头只能扫见繁忙的工地全貌，看不清黄色安全帽下的面孔。

那段时间，雷海涛不管多晚回家，都会抽时间看会儿直播，他知道摄像头安在工地的哪个位置，认得出自己和工友们所在的区域，观看时他会关心，兄弟们今天是不是又加班了。有一次，他用手划出一块区域，指给妻子看："这是我战斗的地方。"

See You Again, Fire and Thunder Brothers

Before leaving the Leishenshan Hospital in Wuhan, a group of construction workers held a small party on March 30, 2020 for fellow worker Xu Dejun for his 32nd birthday. The workers had only just got to know each other on this project. In fact, the owner of the labor service company had only learned about Xu's birthday because of Xu's ID card he handed in.

Nearly 20 workers came to the party, including a worker named Zhou Kai, who paid for the cake out of his own pocket. Though most cake shops had been closed in Wuhan during the novel coronavirus epidemic, he finally found one online and paid 380 yuan for a 14-inch cake. Hearing that Xu Dejun liked playing mahjong, he chose a "mahjong cake" with chocolate mahjong "tiles."

In an empty factory near the hospital, the workers had their party where they drank beer, ate peanuts, danced, laughed and sang birthday songs. Some pasted small Chinese five-star red flags on their faces, left behind after a previous send-off for some of the out-of-town medical staff. Only a day earlier, those temporary medical teams serving at Leishenshan Hospital were told to return to their hometowns, an indication that the epidemic had been alleviated.

Normally, Xu Dejun was a manager of a construction company, and deals with workers on construction sites all year. But for this project, he

See You Again, Fire and Thunder Brothers
火雷兄弟，江湖再见

was just a worker. At his birthday party, he made his entry as designed by his workmates, swaggering into the place and raising his head and holding a cigarette in his mouth. He then sang "My Good Brother" with everyone. He said it was "the most unforgettable birthday" of his life.

Co-worker Xu Xinyan filmed the party and edited it into a short video with the words "See You Someday" at the end. He liked this very much and thought it was "chivalrous."

Another workmate Zhong Weiwei said that everyone there was a comrade-in-arms, and they had all experienced life and death together.

The city of Wuhan was locked down beginning on January 23 in 2020 due to the epidemic. The city made the decision to quickly build temporary hospitals to treat coronavirus patients — Huoshenshan Hospital and Leishenshan Hospital (meaning Fire God Mountain Hospital and Thunder God Mountain Hospital in Chinese). The construction company was the China Construction Third Engineering Bureau Group Co., Ltd. The company's general manager Chen Weiguo said that a total of 35,000 workers participated in the construction, of which nearly 20,000 were from other places. The workers were managed by different labor service companies and had come from different places to the construction site. This caught the attention of people from all over the country. The hospitals were finished in 10 days. By April 15, when the two hospitals closed, a total of 5,071 patients had been treated there.

During their breaks at the construction site, workers from all over the country would get a chance to get to know each other, usually beginning with the offering of a cigarette and then asking, "So where are you from?" and "How many people in your family?" and "Where are you going after this job?"

"Where do you think the next site will be?" was the most discussed topic among the workers. If the epidemic had not happened, they would have been building tall buildings, subways or bridges in different places. Their vehicles were always filled with cutting machines, electric drills, pliers, screwdrivers, and other tools. They are always prepared to move quickly to wherever they find work.

At the Huoshenshan and Leishenshan construction sites, people of different professions could be seen everywhere: civil servants, truck drivers, primary school teachers, business people and deliverymen.

Zhong Weiwei, a native of Wuhan, came here with his father, brother, uncle and cousin. He liked working at the site. He could see the sky when he looked up. When he wanted to sing, he could shout a few words. Around him were all such working-class people, people who didn't have to be "proper."

The 32-year-old had been working at construction sites since he was 15. He grew up in Wuhan, helping build its schools and subway tracks. He also helped build the Qingshan Yangtze River Bridge — the eleventh bridge in Wuhan — which was scheduled to open by the end of the year. His job was in the "hanging basket" dozens of meters over the Yangtze River which constantly rushed beneath him, day and night.

When the boss of the labor service company was looking for people to help build the hospitals, Zhong Weiwei and his brother Zhong Xinxin immediately agreed. They went to the Huoshenshan construction site the next day, worked for two days, and then rushed to the Leishenshan site 32 kilometers away.

On his fifth day working at Leishenshan, Zhong Weiwei was suddenly moved. He'd been standing on the roof, still under construction. He looked out and saw all the heads below him working, and he suddenly burst into tears. "I was touched by how united we Chinese had become. I rarely get emotional, but it really moved me." Tens of thousands of workers were at the site, all wearing the same reflective clothes and yellow safety helmets. At first, foremen could not identify the 40 to 50 workers on their teams, so they asked everyone to write their team's name on their helmets. Finally, foremen could recognize their team members by their eyes.

Lei Haitao is a 43-year-old physical education teacher at No. 5 Middle School in Jiangxia District, Wuhan. His job at the site was to provide logistical support for more than 30 workers. Every morning, he'd call everyone together to assemble before work in the same way he'd teach his class, by shouting out "At ease!" and "Attention!" The workers respectfully referred to him as Teacher Lei.

His duties involved helping in any way he could. At the Leishenshan site, one truck in particular had become very important as a resting place, a warehouse and as a kitchen. He had persuaded the truck driver to stay at the site so that the tired workers could rest in his truck. Also, the truck had quickly become a makeshift warehouse for keeping cables, wires, and construction tools. In addition to this, there was no boiled water at the site, but there were hot water kettles in the truck as well as instant noodles and snacks purchased from small shops nearby.

To save an additional half hour for the workers to rest, Lei would go to the canteen to queue up in advance at noon every day to buy box lunches for the workers. Lei was also responsible for recording attendance and fetching construction tools from the warehouse, which would take more than 20 minutes to walk back and forth. Even if it was just a paper-knife and a few screws, he would make the trip. For tools he wasn't familiar with, this PE teacher would search for pictures on the internet and then go to the warehouse to find them. When he was free, he would help out as an assistant. He would see some workers so tired that they would fall asleep standing against the wall, and some fell asleep without cleaning their lunch boxes after eating. He watched these scenes with a heavy heart. But he had said that he wanted to do something to help after the epidemic hit the city.

To fight the epidemic, Leishenshan Hospital was expanded three times. It was even receiving patients while construction was underway. After the construction had been finished, workers were still responsible for the maintenance. When the ward built by Zhong Weiwei was completed, skilled workers under 40 years old who could work night shifts were needed for maintenance. The Zhong brothers called up familiar workers in town, and Zhong Weiwei repeated the promise which the company had told him: "If you are infected with the virus, the state will give you treatment; if you die, the state will compensate your family." Nearly 100 people signed up in two days.

"If you get infected, you can get cured. That's life. There's nothing to worry about." When Zhong Weiwei called up Xu Xinyan, Xu felt that it was an honor. "If I'm needed, I will definitely go."

There was one occasion when the outdoor sewerage system malfunctioned, and someone was needed to go underground to pull out the broken pipe, containing the patient's feces and other sewage. Saying nothing, two workers on Zhong Weiwei's team quietly put on protective clothing and went down into the sewer. They had to be especially careful to avoid tearing their protective clothing. One of the workers recalled this. He said when they were told they only had three days to deal with the drainage, his only thought was that the task had to be done. "I didn't think too much about it."

Seeing the workers tired and squatting on the ground, nurses would bring out stools, fruit, milk and cakes for them. When one worker was working and needed a hand, some patients helped him by passing him tools. Others would bow or give a thumbs up.

Xu Xinyan has been fond of painting since childhood. He would paint when he was bored, just to kill time. He'd paint pictures of friends, scenes of his hometown, and portraits of celebrities. He never had a teacher to teach him, and learned by watching tutorials on the internet. While working at the Leishenshan site, he saw the medical staff drawing cartoons on the white wall of the hospital corridor, so he also began to draw. He painted the novel coronavirus like a monster with a sickle fighting against the mixer trucks and excavators at the site. Medical staff from different places asked him to draw landmark buildings from their hometowns. The staff of the China Construction Third Engineering Bureau Group asked him to draw cartoon images of the workers, such as a group of workers holding shields portrayed as the "Avengers," named "Anti-epidemic Alliance." During this period, he completed around 20 paintings along the 200-300 meter-long walls of the ward. Workers said they felt relaxed when seeing them. "When people walk through there, they have no fear." These paintings reminded Xu Dejun that everyone had "really joined in the construction of the hospital or played a part in fighting the epidemic."

February 8 was Lei Haitao's last day at the site because he needed to teach his students classes online. He still keeps in contact with his former workmates, and some workers drove to chat with him after the end of the construction.

One worker remembered hearing that a child once called his father at the construction site and asked, "Are you a hero?" The father replied, "Who is a hero?" The son replied, "The medical staff."

Construction worker Zhao Quanxi traveled a long way to come to Wuhan to help with the construction. When local workers heard that he had come such a long way, they were appreciative and took pictures with him, which greatly moved Zhao Quanxi. When the work was finished and he returned to his hometown, friends praised Zhao as a hero.

"Maybe in a few years, other things like this could happen," he said. "If something happens to us, people will come to help us. But once is enough for a plague like this, and I hope it never happens again."

Because he helped build the hospitals, Zhong Weiwei appeared in the TV news. He admitted that he was so happy that he couldn't sleep for two nights. The video lasted 5 minutes and 15 seconds, and he said he watched it no less than fifty times. "Only celebrities and entrepreneurs are newsworthy, not construction workers like us," he said.

Worker Tian Kui became a hero to his daughter. After posting the location of Leishenshan Hospital on his WeChat Moments, he received a "thumbs-up" from the parents of his daughter's classmates in primary school, who called him a hero. His daughter proudly told her classmates that her father was a construction worker in Wuhan.

Lei Haitao realized the significance of the work they had all been doing in Wuhan. "We have struggled, contributed to the people of Wuhan, and have done our best. These workers can tell their children and grandchildren about the work. They don't want any honor, but just something to remember … like a souvenir." Lei Haitao discussed this with the boss of the labor service company a few times, and the two reached an agreement: to make a commemorative medal for each person in the company who worked at the sites.

On April 21, after the two hospitals were closed, a worker received a postcard. On the back was a portrait of a worker and the words "Salute to the Most Beautiful Builder," and on the front was a few lines of praise, ending with "Thank you, Fire and Thunder Brothers! We salute these ordinary heroes!" It was signed by "Huoshenshan Hospital and Leishenshan Hospital Construction Headquarters of China Construction Third Engineering Bureau Group Co., Ltd." He took a photo of the postcard and shared it in his WeChat group.

The construction of the two hospitals received nationwide attention, and the workers were often seen in live broadcasts watched by tens of millions of people online. However, the camera could only capture the whole picture of the busy construction site, and not the faces beneath the yellow helmets.

For Lei Haitao during that time, no matter how late he came home, he would take time to watch the live broadcast. He knew where the camera was installed and could recognize the area. When he watched, he would think about whether his fellow workers were working overtime again that day. As his wife watched with him one night, he pointed out an area on the screen and said to her, "This is where I fought."

出版策划：王君校　韩　晖
统筹协调：付　眉　韩　颖　彭　博
策划编辑：张　超
责任编辑：杨　晗
英文编辑：吴爱俊
封面设计：袁长新
排　　版：北京几何创想艺术设计有限公司
印刷监制：汪　洋

图书在版编目(CIP)数据

平凡老百姓：把日子过出精气神儿 / "最美中国人"丛书编委会编著. -- 北京：华语教学出版社, 2021.11
（最美中国人）
ISBN 978-7-5138-2193-3

Ⅰ.①平… Ⅱ.①最… Ⅲ.①人物—先进事迹—中国—现代 Ⅳ.①K820.7

中国版本图书馆CIP数据核字(2021)第185542号

平凡老百姓：把日子过出精气神儿

"最美中国人"丛书编委会　编著

*

©华语教学出版社有限责任公司
华语教学出版社有限责任公司出版
（中国北京百万庄大街24号　邮政编码100037）
电话：(86)10-68320585, 68997826
传真：(86)10-68997826, 68326333
网址：www.sinolingua.com.cn
电子信箱：hyjx@sinolingua.com.cn
北京虎彩文化传播有限公司印刷
2022年（16开）第1版
2022年第1版第2次印刷
（汉英）
ISBN 978-7-5138-2193-3
006900